Praise for A

MW01256313

"In *A Touch of Light,* Ann Naimark chronicles the spiritual and emotional journey that changed the trajectory of her life. But you will not just follow her journey. This will be your journey. You'll be inspired by Ann's story as she points the way to love of self and all of Creation—the way to a whole new you."

— Dr. Allen Steven Lycka
   Best Selling Co-Author with Jack Canfield of
   The Pillars of Success
   SmartLivingology | Quilly Award Winner |
   3x Best Selling Author
   Keynote and TEDx Speaker | 3x bLU Speaker

"In *A Touch of Light,* Ann Naimark shares her journey to Source and extends a personal invitation to ignite or reignite your own journey to an authentic connection to Love and your True Self."

— Eva Gregory
   Author of *The Feel-Good Guide to Prosperity*

"*A Touch of Light* by Ann Naimark helps people who are on a life journey to find themselves. It guides us through the importance of connection to family, faith, and friendships, and helps us share our deepest secrets, painful moments, and life celebrations. We grow by participating in Ann's growth along her journey. I found myself honoring my relationships and the joy of living through this world's challenges as I prepare for my journey into heaven after fulfilling my earthly purpose. The inspiration and insights Ann shares help us help humanity, our connectivity, and ourselves! This wonderful book is full of life wisdom and stories of the generations that created Ann's lived experience."

— Barby Ingle
   President, International Pain Foundation

"Read *A Touch of Light* and let Ann take you on a wonderous journey as she walks you through her life, her awareness, and her magic. There is a distinct and lovely unfolding that occurs through this read and you will find yourself unfolding with it."

— Donna Bond
Spiritual Life and Business Coach,
Catalyst Personal Transformation

"Ann Naimark's *A Touch of Light* is a fascinating read! Her adventurous spirit has explored life to the fullest and guided her to experience the Light, Laughter, and Love that have enabled her to grow in Joy and Oneness with all of Creation. Ann is deep— intimately connected to Source, with a powerful intuition that transcends the limits of the three-dimensional world that most humans consider to be all there is to reality, until they are called home. Ann has found that none of us is ever really alone. We are all connected—not just with our families and friends, but with all Beings, with the Universe itself, and with Source. We are all one with the Creator! Ann dances with Angels and Ancestors. Her story invites us all into the joyful dance!"

— Ron San Miguel
Author of *Modern Day Mystic: Journey of a Song Catcher*

"*A Touch of Light* is an engaging, insightful journey that offers authentic storytelling integrated with the path to a spiritual awakening. In it, you can find your capacity to access inner wisdom, peace, and joy, and learn to follow your subtle nudges, allowing you to grow to your ultimate potential. This is a beautiful, unfolding read I strongly recommend as you strive to uncover your personal version of home."

— Helen Horyza
Author of *Elevate Your Career: Live a Life You're Truly Proud Of*

"In *A Touch of Light,* Ann Naimark weaves the fabric of her Spirit-infused life and meditation reflections with extraordinary vignettes of her amazing life experiences. She not only provides a sense of what touched her life but also engages you through her ability to connect with your mind and touch your feelings and your spirit—for your own personal growth. This is a book that will make you think and be curious about your own life, and help you find your Self."

> — Janine Naus
> Author of *Creating Heaven Wherever I Am*

"Coming from a conventional upbringing, Ann Naimark's life has been far from conventional. The outer events of her life in this autobiography are interesting and highly entertaining to follow, but more important and inspiring are the discovery and unfolding of her spiritual self. She has the gift of finding light in the darkness and seeing the movements of Spirit, even in mundane events. I believe the reader will gain more insight into how to do the same."

> — Steve Phillips, MA, L.Ac.

"Ann Naimark's *A Touch of Light* is part memoir and part psychology, with the driving force of a personal spiritual quest. It's written with a conscious, discriminating mind and a higher source of insight. Joyful and enlightening."

> — Sandra Warne, MA, LMFT

"*A Touch of Light* is a reflective book that will steer the reader toward insights into their own journey with family, the unknown, travel, and light. Only read it if you want to be inspired."

> — Lisa J MacDonald
> Step It Up Enterprises

A

TOUCH

OF

LIGHT

Opening to the Love
That Is You and All Creation

ANN NAIMARK

Copyright © 2022 Ann Naimark

All rights reserved. No part of this book may be used or reproduced in any manner without written permission from the author and publisher, except by reviewers, bloggers or other individuals who may quote brief passages, as long as they are clearly credited to the author.

Neither the publisher nor the author is engaged in rendering professional advice or services to the individual reader. The ideas and suggestions contained in this book are not intended as a substitute for professional help. Neither the author nor the publisher shall be liable or responsible for any loss or damage allegedly arising from any information or suggestion in this book.

Capucia LLC
211 Pauline Drive #513
York, PA 17402
www.capuciapublishing.com
Send questions to: support@capuciapublishing.com

Paperback ISBN: 978-1-954920-45-3
eBook ISBN: 978-1-954920-46-0
Library of Congress Control Number: 2022919250

Cover Design: Ranilo Cabo
Layout: Ranilo Cabo
Editor and Proofreader: Kevin C. Neece
Book Midwife: Karen Everitt

Printed in the United States of America

Capucia LLC is proud to be a part of the Tree Neutral® program. Tree Neutral offsets the number of trees consumed in the production and printing of this book by taking proactive steps such as planting trees in direct proportion to the number of trees used to print books. To learn more about Tree Neutral, please visit treeneutral.com.

This book is dedicated to my clients—all of you courageous people who have embarked on a journey into yourself and who trust me enough to share your deepest secrets, painful or otherwise. As you grow, you contribute to my growth. Your insights and successes bring me joy and awe as I marvel at your dedication to yourself. You are amazing humans, and I am grateful and honored to have journeyed partway with you.

And to my son, all his wonderful friends, and to all young people—that includes a heck of a lot of folks these days, as I walk down the corridor of my seventh decade! You have all taught me so much. I hope this tome gives back to you some of what you have given me, and that it helps you navigate some of life's twists and turns. I love you all.

Contents

Introduction

This is my story from being an atheist to being fully committed to Source. Though I grew up in an atheist household, I had a sneaking suspicion when I was in tenth grade, that there might be something more than what my parents said: "There is no God," and "there is nothing more than what our senses can discern," and "when our bodies die, that's it; we're gone."

That felt sense that there might be more to the story was the beginning of a varied journey that took me through many twists and turns. My pursuit has opened me to many spiritual adventures that involve human teachers, nature, and spiritual disciplines, and has ultimately brought me back to myself in relationship with the Other, the energy that is Source, that is Creation.

I found that by following my intuition, that inner sense (I often feel this as a calm nudge in my gut or heart area or sometimes everywhere in my body, mind, and feelings), my life has unfolded in beautiful, growing ways. My physical, mental, emotional, and spiritual health have been guided through responding to this gentle inner Love-tap.

Relationship has been my guide, my goal, and my joy. And my relationship with Source, though dimly felt early on, has been my guidepost.

Because I am somewhat of a stream-of-consciousness writer (I go with the flow, though I can do the linear thing and access that part of my brain if I need to), this composition will have that flavor of moving from one seemingly out-of-context idea to another.

It all makes sense to me, of course, and some of my similarly flowy comrades have said they are comfortable with the style. But my other more organized, logical friends have said they have struggled to follow my gist.

So, in order to make everyone's life easier, I want to explain what you'll find as you read on.

Most of this creation talks about events, people, my feelings, and my thoughts—information about my human life so far.

Interspersed throughout are departures from the facts as I remember them into written excerpts from meditations I have had.

Often when I sit to meditate, I will be moved to write about what I have just encountered. I will often still feel like I'm in my meditative state. These contemplations are meant to give you a brief view of what can be possible for you in meditation.

This is not to say you need to have the same impressions as I do. It's more to show that meditation can open you up in your own unique way to a vast, wonderful world of relationship that supports you, lets you feel loved, helps you release old patterns you're done with, and takes you on a fun adventure.

When you let go and let it flow with intent to enhance your own Source connection, what you encounter will be uniquely yours and what is needed for you at the time.

The challenge is to persist!

Besides mixing in some of my meditation reflections throughout this book, I also sprinkle in questions for you to consider in your own life.

For example, once you have read about a challenge that I embarked upon, I might ask you to reflect on whether anything like that has come up in your own life that you want to address or have already addressed.

My intention is to engage with you—not only to connect with your mind but also to touch your feelings and your spirit. My hope is to support your growth.

From my perspective, everything is spiritual—body, mind, emotions, and spirit. In my personal search for wholeness, I have felt that every part of us interacts and affects every other part of ourselves.

If you don't feel good physically, it's hard to meditate. If you feel very angry or sad, it's hard to think clearly.

When all parts are working well, on their own and together, you have a better chance of doing what you love, being in a loving place, being in a loving relationship with the world, and most of all, embodying the love that you already are.

The ironic thing is that I owe this book to my father, without whom I probably wouldn't have embarked on this writing journey.

Many years ago, he said to me, "Why don't you write the story of your life?" The story of my life is largely wrapped up in my spiritual escapades. Did my father, the atheist, realize that this creation was going to have a spiritual focus?

At that time, I thought, *Really?!? Why?* I couldn't imagine that anyone would be interested in my rather ordinary life. And it is an ordinary life.

But somehow, years later, I began to have an idea to do just that.

I researched people who help aspiring authors in their writing process and came upon Christine Kloser. I signed up for her Get Your Book Done program in 2019.

I joined her Facebook group and wrote a post referencing my father, who had died in 2015, saying that I felt his presence, his support for this project.

Christine responded that she also felt him and that she got chills when reading my post.

I didn't write anything at that time, though the thought of the book would now and then surface in my mind.

That is until I was having lunch with my friend Ron in San Francisco. We both were saying that we wanted to write about our lives, with a focus on the spiritual aspects.

Ron told me about a nun he knew who had told him, "If you want to write, just AIC." That is, get your "Ass In Chair" and do it.

So, we decided to support each other by referencing AIC.

Of course, true to form, at first, I didn't do any of Christine's program lessons that aim to guide you through the book writing process, making it easier and better.

Part of me was thinking, *Not another class!* So, I resisted and just started writing. (Ron was going at it the same way, so I had a partner in rebellion).

I was also feeling support from Source to just get the rough draft down.

All during the writing, I felt support from Source, experienced during meditation or at random moments during the day. Sometimes I would feel a positive urging to write from folks on other levels that I identified as Higher Level Positive Light Beings.

Meanwhile, I also wanted to figure out how I would get it published. I listened to Christine talk about publishing avenues and knew right away I wanted her publishing company to be my publisher. I signed up.

And then, when I figured I was close to done, I emailed my Book Guide to Christine's team. She told me that was great! "And here," she said, "is what you need to do before submitting to our editors."

At this point, to know how to finish my part of the manuscript, I had to do Christine's lessons. All fifty-three of them. And I couldn't skip ahead. They had it set so that you had to complete one before the system would let you move on to the next.

My rebel self was being challenged.

I learned a lot, obviously. And not just about book publishing.

I feel that this joyful discovery never ends. And as one who loves adventure, I will keep on keeping on.

With love for you, dear reader, I hope there is something from this manuscript that speaks to you, nurtures you, and gives you ideas for your spiritual adventures.

This Time Around Earth Family

W ell, I finally sat down to write the story of my life.
My friend Ron is somewhere on page 200 of his life story. We decided we would support one another in writing using the initials AIC (Ass in Chair). This acronym came from a nun he knew who told him the best way to get writing done was AIC. So, he has been writing diligently and I haven't. Until now.

I have no idea why I started today. Oh yes, maybe I do.

I signed up with a beautiful lady, Eva Gregory, to get guidance and uplifting energy for my human spiritual evolution. She channels the guides, Theos. These beautiful beings are Streams of Divine Consciousness who have been helping us uncover our True Selves or our Divine Souls. Or how ever you want to phrase it.

The whole point is to evolve into the best us we can be—way beyond what we imagine.

The first meditation that they took us through was two days ago. We are to listen to the meditation every day for a week.

When I went into my email to access the link to the recorded meditation, I couldn't find it. I looked in spam, in trash, through the inbox. Nothing.

I clicked on all the icons in the FB group. Nada.

So, I asked Theos for help.

You may be wondering why I so nonchalantly talk about communicating with something other than humans who speak with a mouth using vocal cords.

That I refer to these others as guides or streams of Divine Consciousness.

That I ask them questions. Or that I so easily say I hear them.

You may wonder if I'm a bit off and decide this book is not for you.

But bear with me if you will. You might find something here that you can relate to in your own life.

Maybe there's something you've felt or seen or heard that you've never told anyone because you dismissed it as nothing or as imagination. Did you wonder about it, though?

If you decide to read on, you might find some of your own experiences written here or something like them.

I want to tell you how I have come to talk to unseen energies, how I discern what energies are trustworthy and not out to mess with us, and why I trust what I hear or sense as appropriate answers.

To my conscious knowledge, it all started when I was fifteen.

I was born into an atheist household. Both parents said God was made up by humans to make themselves feel better.

I think my parents were reacting to what they had read in books about religions, and to their own life experiences. They felt religions were based on fantasy and a need to control people and were a way to exercise power. I don't disagree with some of this. But I have experienced that within each religion there is grace and truth when you take the politics and control out of it.

I imagine that my parents hadn't experienced what I had: a strongly felt sense of something good that I didn't normally feel.

Dad's Parents

My dad, the scientist, came from two atheist parents, Jews who came to America to escape Tsarist Russia. They were intellectual, bohemian, artistic free thinkers. Among other adventures, they sold trains in Europe.

My grandad was an artist who painted sets for Broadway shows in New York. He was larger than life—funny, smart, loving, and full of enthusiasm for so many things.

He always came to visit us from New York bringing dill pickles, Russian black bread, and a salami. He always said you bring a salami to someone you love.

He loved words. When he came to visit (after his wife, Mary, died), we would sometimes play a word game called Categories. To play the game, we made a template on a piece of paper. Across the top, we wrote a five-letter word, each letter being at the head of a vertical column. Down the left side of the paper were five categories, like "artists," "books," or "famous leaders." We drew lines top to bottom and left to right, creating twenty-five squares. In each square, we were to write a word from each category that started with the letter corresponding to each column. So, at the top might be the five-letter word "style." Filling in the category of "artist" starting with the letter "S" might be Swinden (Albert). (I had to look him up!) We were timed—maybe twenty minutes was all we got to fill in our twenty-five squares.

This was not my strong suit! But dad and granddad and mom filled in most of their squares, as I recall.

My granddad and dad would debate vociferously about the veracity of each other's entries. No obscure entry would remain unchallenged! There was lots of laughter and great fun.

My brother Rich remembers this story. Granddad's neighbor worked in the print room at the *New York Times*. During a particularly competitive game with him, Granddad filibustered a whole story about "General Albuquerque" being authentic, and the argument went on for a long time.

On the following Sunday, Granddad picked up his paper outside the apartment door and started yelling "Little One!" (That was his pet name for his small-in-stature second wife.) He called my dad, and who knows who else. To his amazement, his friend had printed it up with a dummy story about General Albuquerque! Must have been fun games.

We lived in New Jersey, an hour west of Manhattan. When my Grandma Mary was alive, she and Granddad lived in the Bronx.

In the 1950s and '60s, Coney Island was the go-to amusement park. Once, we went there with Granddad. Three rides stand out for me: the Steeplechase, the parachute jump, and a small Ferris wheel where you could control the trajectory of the enclosed cage you sat in.

Granddad, dad, me, and my brother Rich rode the Steeplechase. The ride consisted of several metal horses on a track. Riders hopped on, completely untethered and with no safety equipment. The track was powered up and the horses raced around a large building. (It has since been updated to be safer because, in the original version, riders were being thrown off the horses going around dangerous curves.)

Rich and I sat toward the heads of our horses (there was room for two people on each horse) with Dad and Granddad taking the back seats on our respective saddles. I remember a couple of curves that were really scary where we were pulled powerfully to the outside. Dad said he and Granddad were also quite frightened and held onto us super tightly.

My Grandma spoke ten languages. She had a radio program in San Francisco teaching people Russian. I remember her as gentle and loving.

She was mentioned in a book written after World War II, *Why They Behave Like Russians*, by John Fischer. The book talked about her part as an interpreter in the UN aid mission to Russia after the war. Russia had been devastated by Germany, losing more people than were killed in the concentration camps.

My Grandma was feisty. One incident described in the book was of her (all of four feet, ten inches) strongly admonishing a Russian soldier when his behavior was not respectful. He yielded to her fierce correction.

Mom's Parents

My mom's mother's name was Marie. She was a loving grandma, cooked great meals, had a wry sense of humor, and was devoted to her family, whom she worked hard to take care of.

Her pantry was fascinating. It had so many canned goods. (We didn't have a pantry.) And the step stool used to reach cans on top shelves was so cool! You had to unfold the three-step stool, an engineering delight to her grandchildren.

There was a swinging door separating the kitchen from the dining room, something we had never seen. We loved swinging it open from the kitchen to the dining room and back. Magical! At times, we were admonished to not knock into people carrying dishes of food. We never knocked into anyone, but how could we resist that swing!?

After every dinner at their house, grandma would pass a huge bowl of candy around the dinner table. We were each allowed to take one piece. I always went for the chocolate if any were left. My favorite still today!

In their living room was an old chair, which was the bane of active young ones. It had small wheels and wasn't quite steady. Those of us who needed to keep moving decided to make it a rocking chair. More than once, we ended up rocking so hard we flipped the chair onto its back on the floor, us on the chair back, feet in the air, from vertical to horizontal—sans injury.

My mom's dad came from a family of thirteen kids, not all of whom survived. He became the breadwinner for his mother at the age of thirteen when his dad died. He also served in World War I.

He grew glorious vegetable gardens in the far back yard of their house.

I learned baseball from Grandpa. He loved the Philadelphia Phillies, (near where they lived) who, in one season in the '50s, were losing every game. That didn't matter. Just watching them on the small black and white TV was the fun of it. He taught me about balls, strikes, outs, positions, and all the rules.

There was an enclosed, many-windowed porch where Grandpa stored his games. We spent many afternoons learning all kinds of new board and card games that were played with chips. Again, something new for us. An adventure!

It's funny things you remember. They had a very long clothesline that reached almost the entire substantial width of the backyard and would have sagged in the middle except for the notched wooden staff that held up the line, one end into the earth, the notch supporting the line. So cool!

They had a crabapple tree. We found it a treat to pick ripe crabapples. I found it hilarious every time Grandma pronounced crabapples, so she did it a lot to hear me laugh. She emphasized the "b" so it sounded like "cra-bapples."

They had an unfinished dirt basement. You descended into this dark, damp, mysterious space via a rickety wooden staircase. There was a light down there that you had to turn on via a pull-string once you descended.

I found this kind of scary place also fascinating. What strange and surprising stuff would I find there? I recall old wooden-handled tools and wooden boxes. I didn't stay down there too long.

4

My Mom

My mom grew up Presbyterian. Her family wasn't that religious. Sometime in college, I think she questioned her faith.

She was highly intelligent. Her high school teachers told her parents that they should send her to college. They weren't going to. She was a girl. So, because the teachers told them mom should go, her parents sent her.

In college, her English professor said he had never read a better writer. She also learned Spanish which came in handy in her later social justice work. She, like my dad, felt that all people should be given equal rights and helped to succeed in life. That meant *all* people, not just whites.

She was interested in theater, music, and all the arts, as was my dad. She grew up playing the piano and singing.

Growing up, I accompanied Mom to Newark several times where her Spanish was useful when she was advocating for and working with Puerto Rican and Black families, helping them with finding work and accessing services.

When I was born, my mom was quite agoraphobic. She was scared to leave the house. We never quite knew how she came to be so frightened. But later she was able to overcome a lot of her fear and speak at the New Jersey legislature, again advocating for the poor.

Further working to grow herself, she took the Erie Lackawanna and PATH trains into New York City to NYU, where she earned her master's degree in urban planning.

After her kids were raised, she also hosted and produced a cable TV show called *Senior Scene*, where she interviewed interesting seniors. Dad was profuse in his accolades for her interviewing ability.

5

My Dad

Dad attended an accelerated high school in New York City. He graduated at sixteen and went on to Bucknell in Pennsylvania, where he and my mom met.

He then went to the University of Delaware for his PhD in biochemistry.

After working for a pharmaceutical company and a New York advertising agency, he decided to branch out on his own. He started his own advertising company in New York City. He and his partner were in business for many years, advertising for pharmaceutical and scientific instrument companies.

He traveled the world visiting clients, often accompanied by my mom. He gave lectures on what he knew about pharmaceuticals and scientific instruments, to name a couple of subjects.

He participated in think tanks and start-up companies and wrote quite a few articles for magazines.

His first book was *A Patent Manual for Scientists and Engineers*. He authored a number of books after that, such as *How to Be a Truly Rotten Boss*, *Cleaning Out My Attic* (vignettes from his life), and his last book, *The Leadership Disaster*.

His writing was peppered with humor. One short article was entitled "How to Lead a Meeting." It was all tongue-in-cheek and hilarious.

He had great enthusiasm for inventing puns. Your requirement after the pun made its debut was to emit the requisite groan. That was all he needed as perfect acknowledgement of his new creation.

He loved exploring all cultures, especially their food. We sampled strange fare from different countries that he brought home from New York, like the hundred-year-old egg (I think my siblings and I agreed it was disgusting), sea urchins, and fried grasshoppers and worms. (Those were edible. They tasted like potato chips. I brought them to my elementary school class for show and tell and to see which brave souls would sample them.)

He collected the seventeen-year cicadas when they emerged from their nap and fried them. And we ate them. Good protein!

6

There is More to This Life Than Meets the Eyes, Ears, Taste, Smell, and Touch

In my journey with Light, I learned years ago that there are Light Beings on dimensions other than this three-dimensional world. (Check out quantum physics, which talks about multiple dimensions.)

Some are conscious, evolving folks like us, at many levels of awareness. Some have never had a physical body. Many of them are well-intentioned and are here to help. (It's always good to discern where your information is coming from).

With your calling them by name or even generally asking, they are completely, 100 percent, available to you. If you have a question, they will respond. The response may not always be direct, like an idea in your head. It may show up as a sign you see on the road.

When I first heard of this, the idea seemed absurd. What? From a thought or an audible question, there were actual unique people in unseen realms who were of good intent and wanted to help us? They could actually hear us? And if they did, they would answer us somehow? Crazy.

Over time, though, I experienced just that. They can be called Divine Light Beings or Angels or Ascended Masters or Elohim and other names. They are Source-created helpers, the beautiful Divine Family of Source. My relationships with them (and of course, with Source) developed gradually. This section of the book will unfold my frolic from the seen to the unseen.

Light Meets You Where You Are

Apparently, I've always been enamored with Light.

As a nine-month-old, I developed croup. My coughing was hard, raspy, and frequent.

My parents were beside themselves, not knowing what to do. At one point, a doctor told them to put kerosene in the back of my throat to stop the coughing. It kind of helped.

But what helped stop the coughing the most was light.

It was Christmas. And my parents had put up a Christmas tree with many colored lights. When I was in the middle of an awful hack, my dad would carry me to the tree and point out the lights. As I looked at them, I immediately stopped coughing, mesmerized and still.

Later, at the age of fifteen, I remember sitting outside in our backyard, musing about my parents' atheist belief. During that contemplation, I had a whole-body calm, a sense that maybe they didn't really know the truth about spiritual matters.

After all, my dad was a scientist. To him, what his five senses and scientific method revealed was the truth. If he couldn't see it or prove it, it wasn't so.

He might have had more receptivity if he had spent that weekend with Einstein as a teenager. My grandfather knew Einstein, who offered to hang out with his son, who was then fifteen or sixteen years old.

Dad spoke with regret about missing that opportunity. He said he was such a *cool* teenager that he didn't want to hang out with a grownup!

But even so, Einstein sent him an autographed photo that said, "To George." It hung in our hallway for years.

8

We Grew Up with All Kinds of Art

Mom and dad loved music, especially classical, jazz, and musicals.They would go check out a Broadway play and if it was appropriate for their kids, they would go a second time and take us. Shows were much cheaper then!

We saw *Peter Pan, My Fair Lady, Hello Dolly, Fiddler on the Roof, Guys and Dolls*, and more, with their original casts.

At *Peter Pan*, we had a box seat. I was about six years old. We were on a level with Peter (Mary Martin) as she flew around the stage on the wires. Probably like every six-year-old kid, that's what I wanted to do!

Watching Julie Andrews sing and the chorus dance in *My Fair Lady*, I wanted to join them on the stage. I think it was 1954 and I was still six. I would join many choirs in my life, and I have always loved to dance!

9

We Explored Nature

My parents took us on many interesting family summer vacations. Getting to Nova Scotia took one long car ride. (Are we there yet?!) We fished and caught a load of pollock—great eating after being cooked over the campfire. We also picked up mussels and snails on the beach (clean in those days) and steamed them for dinner.

For two summers, we drove to the Thousand Islands on the St. Lawrence River, where we stayed in a houseboat my dad rented.

My family would explore the islands and my dad and brother would fish for our dinner. My dad, proudly wearing his captain's hat, learned to pilot the houseboat and navigate the sometimes-roiling waters of the river.

I had learned to sail at a month-long camp and loved it. One windy day, I took our "soap dish," as we called it, an eleven-foot Styrofoam sailing dingy, out from the houseboat to sail across the river.

During my voyage, the wind got stronger—so strong that I was unable to come about (do a one-eighty to turn around and go back to the houseboat). I tried and tried to turn the boat around, but it was too small, and the wind was too fierce and kept pushing me across the river. So, I decided to just beach the boat on the opposite shore and wait till the wind died down.

After a while, a kindly resident in a motorboat came to my rescue. He asked if I wanted a tow. Much to my chagrin, as I didn't want to admit defeat, I said yes. Who knows how long I would have sat there? So, he towed me back to the houseboat. My dad said I didn't look happy. I wasn't! I was supposed to have conquered this on my own!

Apparently, I have always wanted to do things by myself. My mom talked about her trying to help me with new tasks when I was a toddler. I would often inform her that I was doing this "by self!"

What's your relationship to challenges that come up in your life? Do you want to go it alone? Ask for help? Your way is your way; none are better.

Another piece of memory popping up from houseboat enterprises.

I had brought a black kitten home one day that someone had thrown out of a car. My argument was: *We need this kitten.* So convincing! But the parents agreed.

That summer, we brought our little black kitty with us on the houseboat. Well, the houseboat would rock and roll with the swell of the river, bringing water onto the deck. One day the kitten disappeared overboard. We were frantic. Everyone ran every which way around the massive boat, peering into the water below. No kitten. We feared the worst.

My mom went to the opposite side from where the kitten had submerged, put her arm in the water, and—miracles of miracles—the kitten climbed up her arm and out of harm's way. She had incredibly swum the whole width of the boat (probably ten feet) underwater. Bedraggled and in shock, she was nonetheless fine. We didn't let her out of our sight after that. And, in hindsight, who takes a kitten on a houseboat? Adventurous or ill-advised?

But this was the dad we grew up with—adventurous but taking chances that didn't seem too crazy.

My dad's father was a creative artist and free thinker with sometimes wild ideas.

When my dad was about three years old, his father decided that it would be awesome to get one of those gigantic weather balloons, go to Coney Island, get a very long, sturdy rope, tie one end of the rope to the balloon, and wind it around his small son while he held the other end.

And with the gusty winds off the beach, my very small father would sail high in the sky on the end of a weather balloon. Granddad thought it would be such fun!

Alas, it was not to be. My fierce, wise grandma roundly shot down the whole hare-brained idea. Her three-year-old son wasn't going anywhere hanging in mid-air off a weather balloon over the ocean!

So, I come by loving adventure honestly. It's in my genes.

How do you relate to the Unknown? Is it scary or exciting? An adventure?

Out of the Nest: Adventure and Light Bites

I went to college at Hobart and William Smith in Geneva, New York. I had many firsts in college, including losing my virginity (which was not exciting). I had three boyfriends, two of whom wanted to marry me. But they were going into the military, and I couldn't for the life of me imagine being a military wife. When I thought about the regimen and being a wife of a military man, my body, mind, and spirit revolted.

My dad had been in the Navy in WWII in the Philippines running a radio station, and we heard many stories of his escapades there. So, I wasn't against the military.

But this was 1968. We were in the middle of the Vietnam War with protests all over the country and the world. Students and police tangled violently. Martin Luther King, Jr., was killed in April. Robert F. Kennedy was killed in June.

On my campus at Hobart and William Smith in Geneva, New York, we were visited by Tommy the Traveler, as he came to be known. He was hired by the FBI and police to incite violence on the campus. He had been to some SDS (Students for Democratic

Society, a left-wing group) meetings in the area. He was encouraging students to bomb the ROTC building. He taught them how to fashion a fuse for a bomb and discussed which was better, a firebomb or black powder.

Two hundred students found out that Tommy was a plant and confronted the police. We made national news.

I was aware of this after the fact. Our campus was tense.

During that year I was talking to a friend, JoAnn, about traveling in Europe during the next summer. We got very excited by the idea and were not deterred by the violence that was gripping the country. Probably we needed some way to relieve the tension we were feeling.

I wasn't too excited about getting involved in violent protests, but I was totally against the war in Vietnam and supported civil rights 100 percent. My brother had decided that if he were drafted, he would go to Canada, which I completely endorsed.

JoAnn and I came up with a plan. I would go to England first and then meet up with her in Milan, Italy. Then we would travel together, maybe with her sister, to Austria, Germany, Holland, and then back home.

I had $500 or so in the bank. I was twenty. I researched flights to Europe for students and found one from the American Youth Hostel organization for $265, round trip, from New York to London, and back from Amsterdam to New York.

It also featured a stay in Tiptree, England, at an international farm camp. The main draw there was that you got to meet people from across the globe. Tiptree makes famous strawberry jam and students from all over the world would book time there and pick strawberries in their fields, earning some extra cash as farm laborers.

I booked the flight and a two-week stay at Tiptree.

My plan was to finish out my two weeks, then travel across the Channel to Paris. From there, I would take a train to the south of France and stay with my dad's cousin, Joe, in Antibes for a few days. Then I would travel to Milan to meet JoAnn.

The flight over the Atlantic was exciting. It was my first trip off the North American continent. I didn't sleep (I never can anyway on planes), and we landed in London on an overcast, rainy day during early morning rush hour.

My directions took me to the underground, where I saw all those London businessmen dressed in their typical black suits, coats, and bowler hats, carrying the classic black umbrellas. I was amused.

I found my way to Tiptree, about fifty miles northeast of London, and onto the bus from the farm camp that brought me to my new digs. I was ushered to a building with small rooms where we workers would live. There were two bunk beds and room for little else. The floor space between the bunk beds was about three feet. There were communal bathrooms and showers.

They had a communal dining hall, which doubled as a party and dance room where the management would hold soirees to help us get to know each other.

On my first night, there was a dance. I danced with an Italian man. I spoke no Italian, nor he any English. He got so turned on during the dance that he ejaculated right there on the dance floor. That killed that relationship.

I had three roommates in our tiny bedroom. A woman from Holland became a good friend. She later invited me to her home, where her parents delighted in showing me the sights.

Picking strawberries is hard, backbreaking work. You squat all day, pick up the leaves of the plants to find the berry underneath, pick the berry, pull the calyx (the white part just under the stem) and stem off with your fingernails, and put the berry in a basket. You got paid a couple of bucks for each basket. It was actually a pretty weird setup because you also paid rent on your crash pad. I think the bosses just found a way to not shell out a lot of money for the farm workers.

All of us student workers knew that the Italians were the fastest pickers, partly because they needed the money to get back to Italy when their time was done in the fields. The Americans and Swedish were the slowest, that is, the laziest.

From time to time, the big boss man (as we called him) would come around with his metal leaf picker-upper to see if we were getting all the strawberries. Apparently, they had experience with us vacationing student farm workers.

I became friends with a Swedish student, Stefan, from Tyreso, outside Stockholm. We liked each other and so he invited me to Tyreso after my journey in lower Europe.

I also met a friend, Mary, who lived in Greenwich Village back in the states. She and I got along well together. We decided after a week of farm labor that we were on vacation, and we'd had enough of squatting for eight hours every day.

We decided to cancel our next laboring week and set off hitchhiking west through England for South Wales. She was going to meet her sister in the south of France at a later date.

Hitchhiking these days is obviously fraught with difficulty, but in 1968 in Europe, we encountered kind, wonderful people who went out of their way to help us.

At the same time, my Dutch roommate, Kalie, decided she had also had enough of strawberry picking and left the camp with her Spanish boyfriend.

She invited me and Mary to Cambridge to hang out with them for a day. I still have a picture of Kalie and her boyfriend in a skiff on the river Cam enjoying a leisurely glide.

Mary and I also went to Oxford. I remember the beautiful architecture of the University of Oxford so well. We strolled through the grounds feeling the old history of it all.

Drivers went out of their way to get us hitchhikers to where we wanted to go. Once we got a ride in an old Rolls Royce with a paneled wood interior. We felt special.

We passed through Cardiff in South Wales and passed a sign with the impossible-to-pronounce, abundant-consonant Welsh name, Llanfairwllgwyngyllgogerychwyrndrobwllllantysiliogogogoch, which means "St Mary's church in the hollow of the white hazel near to the fierce whirlpool of St. Tysilio of the red cave." As I write this, I am reminded of the Light Language that comes out of my mouth when leading meditations at times. The language sounds like consonants. (Light Language is just another form of expressing Light—like in a song, a painting, or instrumental music—when you're in a meditative state.)

Finally, we made it to the other side of the Atlantic from New York. Standing on the cliffs near Aberystwyth overlooking the ocean, in the wildness of the rolling hills, I felt something familiar, untamed, magical, and untouched by civilization. This energy invigorated me and left me wanting more. This was one of two places on my Europe trip that touched my heart, body, and mind. I felt peace, love, and home.

Mary and I hitchhiked back through England to Dover, where we caught the ferry to Calais, France, and then took a train to Paris. It was only a month after the fabled Night of the Barricades, when French youth began a student revolt against their autocratic government that eventually led to some 10 million workers going on strike. When police blocked the path of the protesters, the students took cobblestones from the streets and began erecting barricades to protect themselves. The upheaval led to the arrest of hundreds of students and the hospitalization of hundreds more, including police officers. The president even fled the country. Upon his return, there was a new election, and France was changed.

I don't know for sure, but I suspect that the time Mary and I spent in France, coming into the country a month after that unrest and upheaval, was so smooth partly because the people had just gone through a major expression of what had been disturbing them for so long. They had spoken out and they had been heard. Pressure had been released. They had liberated themselves.

Have you had that experience of speaking your truth and feeling free?

When Mary and I arrived in Paris, everything was functioning again: trains were running, and workers were back to work. We arrived at a perfect time for our journey.

We hitchhiked down through the center of France to the Riviera. People were most kind. Our French was pitiful. (I had taken French in high school and college, but my conversational usage was choppy.) People just seemed grateful that we tried.

We got to Marseilles via a truck driver who found us a hotel. Early next morning in the street below, the garbage trucks showed up. What a noisy way to wake up!

That day, we hitchhiked to Antibes (near Nice) where Mary and I parted; she to meet her sister, and I to stay a few days with my dad's cousin Joe, the retired dentist.

He was a most gracious host. He had two daughters around my age. His wife, Georgette, was an artist and he had built a whole studio and private museum for her paintings.

He was also a reputable art photographer who was welcomed into the events of famous artists working on the Riviera, such as Joan Miró, Marc Chagall, and others.

Joe was very excited to bring me to Joan Miró's eightieth birthday party. He, as the photographer, could get us in. I happily agreed to go with him. There were a lot of people there, all excited to be around this famous artist. The party had hors d'oeuvres, cake—most appropriate for a birthday party—and one of his paintings.

I was taken by this short man with sparse, white hair. He was surrounded by admirers, and he just seemed amused. He was in the party but not of it. He saw me and winked. Was he flirting with me? Or just communicating that this was just so much fuss?

Or did my connection to Miró via his wink also energetically presage how I was going to work with therapy clients many years later; seeking to uncover hidden causes of their struggles? Did he somehow sense a fellow delver?

In researching this great artist, I learned that Miró used emotion in his art; he wanted to express the feeling of his depictions. His childlike paintings revealed the complex world of dreams, imagination, and spontaneity. He was an important influence on his Surrealist cohorts.

He was not interested in social conventions, but he wanted to connect with the masses of humanity, to find the common ground. He also had a great sense of humor.

I also came upon an article that said his birthday was April 20, 1968, and that had been the date of his eightieth birthday party. I was puzzled. All these years I thought I was at his birthday party in July 1968. And that's what I have been telling folks all along.

So what party was I at? I thought. *Okay, I'm cracking up.*

As I searched the internet for "Joan Miró birthday," I came upon his "Birth of Day" painting from 1968.

I was at his "Birth of Day" painting reception! I had misheard my dad's cousin.

This autobiography writing clarifies so much!

Joe was also excited to show me an unfinished wall painting by Marc Chagall. It was on an enormous wall inside a building. I loved Chagall, his rich colors, and the feel of his art. To see that was a huge blessing and I was humbled.

I spent a few days with Joe and Georgette and then went on by train to Milan, Italy, where I was supposed to meet JoAnn on a particular day at a particular time. I had her phone number and called several times but got no response.

Since it was getting late, I decided I had better just get on with it and go to Venice, the first stop on our planned leg of the trip, because I had a place to stay. I took a train and at one point during the journey, an Italian train conductor suddenly grabbed my boob and then, just as suddenly, moved on. Shocking. He seemed pleased with himself. I was left physically unharmed but emotionally unhinged. I recovered.

I got to Venice and spent the rest of the day entranced by the Piazza San Marco, the Basilica di San Marco, the music, and the food.

I was chagrined at the absence of contact from JoAnn. Well, I would continue our planned route and see what I could see.

From Venice, I took another train into Austria to Bregenz, a darling town just east of Switzerland. It sports a huge lake named Constance.

Bregenz was home to lots of Catholic churches. On my first night there, I stayed in a convent that doubled as a student hotel. We all slept on cots in a large, cold room, even though it was summer. At 6 a.m., the nuns ushered us out as it was time for them to clean.

What do you do at 6 a.m. in any city? I found open cafes and wandered around, feeling the amazing oldness of the place.

Being a young female American walking alone on the promenade at the lake, of course I would come to the attention of local young Austrian men. One of them, he called himself Charlie, took me for a boat ride on the lake. It was beautiful. We had dinner or lunch; I can't remember which. It was a short-lived connection as I had to move on.

I may have stayed the second night at Pension Sonne (hard to recall exactly) with shared baths and a good breakfast.

It was at breakfast that I came to the attention of another Austrian man, probably in his twenties, who spoke no English. My German was spotty, but I could get the gist of some things.

He was lonely and wanted a companion, so he offered to drive me to Innsbruck. I said I was going on to Germany so I wouldn't be staying around. He drove me anyway, as that was his destination.

The drive was breathtaking, winding around the Alps. This drive was the second time, after South Wales, where I was in awe at the beauty, the majesty of the mountains, and the feeling of something deep and magical touching my soul. I wanted to live there.

(What in your life has affected you deeply in a wonderful way? Might that be something you could return to that could help you relax and let go of stress?)

Innsbruck is an enchanting city, nestled in a valley surrounded by the Alps. My driver put me up at a hotel and took me to the train the next day where I went on to Munich, which is called München in German.

Munich has beautiful parks. I was sitting on a bench in one eating lunch when I was approached by a young German man. He was very kind and a bit nerdy. We had a good conversation, in German and English. He said he was going to the Deutsches Museum and asked if I wanted to join him. That had been part of my plan, so I said yes.

The Deutsches Museum is the world's largest museum of science and technology, with close to 28,000 items. It has about 1.5 million visitors per year.

This museum is absolutely amazing. The one exhibit that stood out the most for me was the aircraft collection, featuring complete airplanes on display. I'm not sure how many there were at the time, but today there are seventy.

My German guide also indicated that I had to test German bier! So later we went to the famous Hofbräuhaus for beer and Bavarian food. The atmosphere was very jovial, and the beer was yummy.

I went to a youth hostel that night having had a lovely taste of German hospitality.

The next day I took a train to Heidelberg, city of romance and churches. The church I remember most had two steeples. I sat in the pews inside and was touched; something sweet inside was stirring.

In Heidelberg, I also experimented with smoking. I thought, *Why not!?* I think I tried it for about five days and then quit. It smelled terrible.

From Heidelberg, I went on to Amsterdam, Holland, on invitation from my friend who had been my roommate in Tiptree—strawberry land.

In 1968, the student hotels, or hostels, were very cheap. I paid $1 per night. We slept in a dorm with other women. And in the morning, they served a huge breakfast.

It was at breakfast that next morning that I heard a loud exclamation behind me: "Ann!" It was JoAnn. She and her sister had also traversed the route that she and I had laid out. And here we finally met!

We exchanged news and knew that we were going on our separate routes. I had a whole other journey mapped out by that time and so did she. So be it. It was kind of fun to meet up with her if only for one breakfast.

The youth hostel was in the red-light district on one of the canals. Prostitution was legal and at night as you promenaded down the street next to the canal, each so-called "storefront" display window showcased the wares within—a red light shining on a scantily clad woman reclining on pillows or comfy couch.

This was something new! I had never seen prostitution in action. And no one batted an eye. This was normal.

I loved Holland. I was blown away by the hundreds of bikes parked everywhere, ridden everywhere, just everywhere! They took over the streets. Cars were secondary.

The big, burly Dutchmen seemed amused noticing this American student being bowled over!

Kalie met me in Amsterdam, and we went for a boat ride on the canals while she told me all about what buildings we were passing and something of the history of the place.

We also visited a memorial to the Jews interned by the Nazis in World War II. I am half Jewish on my father's side, and this was important to me. I felt my first personal experience of heavy grief about the holocaust as I walked around the walls of the memorial. My body felt the dread, the sadness, the hopelessness, and the despair.

My sweet, hospitable former strawberry fields roommate brought me to her home somewhere outside of Amsterdam. Her parents were most gracious. They drove me all around to see the sights of the dykes, the fields, and the lovely countryside.

Her parents had a surprise planned for dinner that night. They were excited. I wasn't to know. The moment came, and lo and behold! They had ordered Chinese. I was properly surprised! And we all enjoyed the Dutch Chinese meal.

In Tiptree, I had palled around with a Swedish student, Stefan. He was in a graduate program for math and was a smart guy with a wry sense of humor. He made fun of the Swedish, the Americans, all were fair game. I enjoyed him.

He had invited me to Sweden, and I had determined to go. He and his parents lived in Tyreso, outside of Stockholm.

To get to Stockholm, I took the twenty-four-hour boat train from Amsterdam. I sat in a compartment with two hilarious English students, who entertained us the whole way. I got no sleep that night!

I arrived in Stockholm early in the morning, got off the train, and was astonished at all the beautiful blonde-haired people. There was also a crystal-clear feeling in the clean air, probably a relief from sitting in an enclosed compartment, breathing air from three other sleepy travelers.

Stefan met me at the station and drove me to his parents' home where he was staying. His family spoke no English and my Swedish was non-existent. I clearly remember his mom coming outside to meet me, talking away a mile a minute while all I could do was nod and smile and thank her in English. I should have asked Stefan how to say "thank you" in Swedish.

I was shown up to my room. Stefan's mom had prepared a huge breakfast in honor of my visit. There must have been five or six plates of yummy pancakes, eggs, meat, vegetables, and things I can't remember. I was embarrassed and a bit alarmed at such a large spread. Was she trying to impress me? Why?

Stefan showed me around the area. We went to beautiful parks and walked around.

His mom continued to ply me with food and talk to me in Swedish which made me uncomfortable and confused.

I was pretty naive. But eventually, I figured out that she wanted me to hook up with her son.

He was nice and all, but I wasn't in love with him.

Eventually, I said goodbye and went back to Amsterdam for my flight home. I don't remember the long trip back to Holland. I probably blocked it out.

I do, however, remember the long night in the Amsterdam airport waiting for my flight to New York because, for some reason, planes were delayed. We lay around on the floor all night, trying to rest.

Those two months in Europe when I was twenty were a big deal for me. Though the trip was hatched out to be a trip with a friend, circumstances had called for me to switch gears mid-trip and go it alone.

I can't remember ever really being afraid. People were so sweet and generous and helpful.

Even though my high school German was scant, I was able to find my way through Austria and Germany, finding places to stay (with the help of my travel book), discovering places to eat, learning what trains to catch, and getting to the train stations on time. I did it. It grew me.

In 1968, students traveled a lot in Europe, so locals were pretty used to seeing us. Student hotels and hostels were easily accessible—and they fed us. All for one or two dollars per night.

During that eight-week summer trip, I spent $500 in total—$265 round trip on the plane, and the rest mainly on lodging, food, and some transportation.

Back in the states, I had a ball relaying my adventures as I showed off my many pictures.

And again, South Wales and Austria were the two places where I felt magic, where my body felt soft, electric, and alive as something about the land (or a memory?) brought me right into the present moment. I felt peace and love, just from being on the land.

What brings you peace, love, and joy?

Those felt memories remain mysteries. And it's perfectly all right. I was to feel those same feelings and more like them as my life unfolded.

As I reflect, remember, and write about my eight-week summer journey in Europe in 1968, my heart swells with gratitude for all the kind-hearted people I met there. They truly made my twenty-year-old vacation a trip to treasure. They helped shape me. I feel nothing but fondness for those in England, Wales, France, Italy, Austria, Germany, Holland, and Sweden.

Without realizing it, I was visiting ancestral domains. My brother did his DNA test and discovered that my mother's side included English, Irish, Scottish, German, Scandinavian, and Iberian Peninsula. Maybe lurking in my DNA memory were heart-filled ancestral adventures, especially in South Wales and Austria.

11

Source Guides You Through Redirections

A digression. When I was applying to college in 1965 and '66, my parents drove me around to several schools on the east coast. When we set foot on Pembroke (the sister to Brown), I was in love. My heart was set on this campus. It may have been the brick buildings.

But it was not to be. I wasn't accepted. In fact, the only college to which I was accepted was Hobart and William Smith. Thank goodness they let me in! I probably set my sights too high, or fate-Spirit intervened to lead me where I needed to go.

As I peruse the present-day Hobart and William Smith website, I am filled with gratitude and pride for this small liberal arts school in upstate New York.

College in Geneva, New York, was snowy and cold in the winter. Some winters, we walked completely bundled up down the hill from dorm to class in two feet of snow, where the wind chill was twenty below.

I started college in 1966. The Sixties, with their sex, drugs, and rock and roll, along with the Vietnam War and protests, were a time of big societal change.

Freshmen in the women's section of the college, William Smith, had to abide by great formality. We had to wear skirts to meals, line up, walk single file to the dining hall, stand behind our chosen seats at round tables that seated about eight, and wait for the headmistress to start grace. After grace, we could sit down.

Sometime during freshman year, the students protested this arcane practice, and we were allowed to wear pants.

As a freshman, my declared major was biology. However, after a year of competing with the twenty-four-hour–per–day pre-med student study habits and getting Cs in biology, chemistry, and physics, I decided this was for the birds! I don't mean to demean birds; rather I should say, this sucked! I wasn't used to getting Cs.

So, in my junior year, I switched my major to psychology. The conscious idea was that it would be easier. Interesting, yes. But I was mainly trying to redeem my ego!

Well, who knew that psychology would be my focus from 1969 to the present day, would facilitate my own mental health, and would ultimately greatly help mature my spiritual journey?

(Because, as I have come to believe, everything is spiritual—body, mind, emotions, and spirit. And I feel that it's important to attend to all these aspects of ourselves in order to evolve.)

The psychology department at Hobart and William Smith had a primarily behavioral orientation. Looking over their website now, it appears that continues in 2020. My most interesting courses were about personality development. Was this a preview of my career?

In high school, when I was in tenth grade, I spent a summer month learning sailing at a Girl Scout camp called Eagle Island in Upper Saranac Lake in New York state.

One fun activity in college was the women's sailing team.

It was fun because I loved to sail. I became captain of the women's team since I had knowledge about sailing. We traveled to other women's colleges for sailing races. We usually came in last, or far back in the final results.

One fine day, we drove to another women's college in New York. I brought my friend, Joanie, to be crew. We sailed boats with two sails—jib and mainsail. I worked the rudder and the mainsail (the bigger sail), while the crew, Joanie, held onto the line controlling the jib (the smaller, front sail).

Joanie knew nothing of sailing. She was enthusiastic and that was all we needed. She also was carrying a bit more weight than me.

I advised her that shifting weight in a light sailboat like ours would empty the wind from the sails and we would lose speed. So, the best thing would be for her to sit in the middle of the boat and stay there.

I remember a lot of laughter between the two of us when she forgot my sage wisdom. She would jiggle around, the sails would flop, and we would lose ground. But we didn't care!

Well, Spirit or nature or something also had a great sense of humor that day.

We were in a race and were in last place. Joanie had gotten the hang of sitting in the middle and staying put. Suddenly, we were overtaken by a steady gust of wind, and, to our joy and amazement, we started gaining ground. We were moving past other boats with ease and grace—no effort. It just happened. We passed every single boat, and we came in first! Joy and jubilation!

As I reflect on this singular event, I can't help but wonder. We were having a great time being last, being second to last. We were giggling a lot. We had let go of needing to win or anything except having fun.

On reflection, I relate it to what I have learned about the energy of Spirit—that joy, humor, letting go, being in the moment, and going with the flow help us reach goals and bring us delicious life surprises.

Can you think of a time when this happened to you?

I am filled with gratitude and pride for this small liberal arts school in upstate New York.

The late U.S. congressman John Lewis, who gave a convocation address to the college in 2007, said, "I have been all over this country to speak at colleges and universities, and let me tell you, there is a sense of community at Hobart and William Smith that I have not seen elsewhere." (Wickenden 2010, 12)

And in his 2008 convocation address, author Eric Liu said, "At the level of the head, and more importantly at the level of the heart, something special is going on at Hobart and William Smith. . . This is a place where service and stewardship are woven into every aspect and every detail of campus life." (Liu 2008)

And I am impressed by how my college has grown!

As of this writing, 60 percent of the students study abroad in almost fifty places in the world, and 96 percent of students talk to their teachers outside of class. No teaching assistants teach classes. Students come from forty states and thirty-five countries. More than fifty languages are spoken on the campus. The community does more than 80,000 service work hours per year and 100 percent of the students participate in this and other community research.

Wow. From my class of 1970 to now, fifty years later, this sweet little college on beautiful Lake Seneca in the Finger Lakes has evolved in the manner of my own heart and head.

12

Watering Source Seeds

I am grateful to the Spirit who has directed my growth and led me to create this account of my earthly life.

As I write and research my own history, I am growing in an understanding of myself. My heart is opening wider. Through revisiting these adventures, I am feeling a deeper connection to myself and an appreciation for the multiplicity of support that molded me.

It leads me to humility.

Post-College and a Meditation for You

After college at age twenty-two, I went to my first Hatha Yoga class. What I loved most was the deep relaxation at the end of class. I found it easy to do and loved the feeling of peace.

A Meditation to Help You Relax

I invite you to enter into the depths of Love as you read these words. As Love has created you, so are you Love.

Allow your body to rest.

Breathe.

Sigh.

Feel all muscles, tendons, bones, organs, eyes, mouth, scalp, cheeks soften.

Breathe again. Let your belly rise and fall with breath. Be your breath.

Let your breath move into your muscles, down your arms, into your torso, down your back, into your legs.

Let everything rest. Pause.

Let your breath enter your head. Let it circulate in soft spiral waves of gentle oxygen to all portions of your brain. Let your brain surrender to the restful oxygen of life.

Be at peace.

Breathe again. Deeply. Into your belly.

Breathe into your heart, center chest. Feel your heart enfolded in the warm arms of Love. Be here.

Now, coming from behind you, let the arms of Love encircle your whole body, mind, and heart, enfolding you, creating deeper surrender, relaxation, into safety and calm.

There is nothing to do but receive.

The Mother of us all invites you.

(Please return to this meditation whenever you desire to re-center into the core of who you are.)

At that time, I worked at the State of Connecticut Welfare Department in Stamford as a caseworker. Ellie was another caseworker. We became friends. She invited me to Puerto Rico for a little vacation.

We went and met a few guys who were into karate. We were impressed with their mastery of the art. One dude especially stood out for me. I developed a crush, and we had a brief encounter.

This occasion was a preview of a later encounter in Puerto Rico.

Back in Connecticut, Ellie introduced me to a couple of friends, Jonathan, and Margaret. Margaret was pregnant. She had prepared so well, was so relaxed about the birth, and the baby was so ready to enter the light of the earth that the baby basically slid out of her in a quick, two-hour labor. I was quite impressed with Jonathan's support of her, her trust in the process, and the feeling of love that permeated their home.

Jonathan acquainted me with weed. In a closed-up Volkswagen Beetle, we smoked a joint. I wasn't that impressed, but I felt something.

After a year at the Welfare Department, I decided that I needed to do something more *me*. What was going to interest me? I thought I wanted to teach kids.

More Education

I applied to and got into the University of Maryland in the Child Studies Department. I took a couple of classes on child development. My goal was to do something with kids, but I didn't exactly know what.

In College Park, MD, I met a guy who was a math genius. He was solving problems that had been puzzling mathematicians for years. That impressed me. He moved into my small house. With his clingy, dependent friend. Ewww.

After my first semester classes were over, I moved out and left College Park and the pair who needed a crash pad. My master's degree in child studies was over.

From babysitting while growing up to being a camp counselor at a day camp and at an overnight camp for blind kids, I knew I liked working with kids.

I also was drawn to alternative schools that had kids getting up and moving around instead of sitting all day and strove to encourage full-person development instead of merely striving for mental acumen. I knew we were more than our brains. We have a body and feelings too. We learn through art and music and movement.

I had participated in a summer program in Cambridge, Massachusetts, in an open classroom school for elementary school kids where we played the role of the kids. We learned how to teach in that setting by experiencing how it was to move from one activity to another, completing tasks designed to support our full growth. That summer, I learned how to throw a pot on a wheel. I loved the internal centering required to make it happen. It was one of my early experiences with meditation.

Has anything in your life brought you into a still, quiet place? Like art or music or nature?

Then I applied to and was accepted to teach in an open classroom school in New York. I was totally unprepared. I hadn't been trained as a teacher. I oversaw ten children, ages six to ten. I had no materials and wasn't even sure what to ask for. They had few resources to provide for us. Suffice it to say it was a disaster. I didn't do any favors for those kids.

A friend at that school, Laura, was listening to the music of Cat Stevens and the Moody Blues. They sang about wonderful energies that we were only just beginning to tune into. The music helped us feel peaceful, loving, and expansive. It helped us deal with our funk at the school.

15

The Vibrancy
That is Source—
Pushing You Out of Your
Comfort Zone

Midyear, Laura was leaving her abusive husband and needed somewhere to go with Sharon, her seven-year-old daughter. Puerto Rico sounded good to me. I still harbored a faint crush on that karate dude, and I was done with the school. I kind of hoped my old crush would help us find a place to stay.

Well, that didn't work out.

When we arrived, I connected with Luis and it sure wasn't the same. It also sounded like he had another Caucasian American woman he was dating. So much for that idea.

So, Laura, in all her intuitive wisdom, announced that we would go east from San Juan to Luquillo, a popular tourist beach area. I was clueless about why but went along.

We arrived in Luquillo, and then Laura felt we should keep walking east. So, we did. On the beach. We hadn't walked too far when we came upon a tent camp of about twenty or so American hippies, camped off the beach under the trees. (Laura's intuition knew something.)

A brother and sister had established themselves as casual leaders of the tribe. They directed the gathering of food in the nearby rainforest and made decisions about other group activities. They ascribed to some spiritual practice and had a developing intuitive sense. They commanded a bit of authority, and everyone seemed content to let them be in charge. These were laid-back hippies after all. Just chillin'.

My four months in Puerto Rico were full of mind-expanding, dangerous, living-on-the-edge adventures.

I experienced parts of life that I might never would have if I had been on the mainland.

First of all, the colors in Puerto Rico were so vibrant. Everything seemed more of itself. Experiences were also that way—more intense, more dramatic, more.

Laura, Sharon, and I lived in a small tent pitched away from the surf among other makeshift shelters.

Living on the beach next to the beautiful blue ocean was incredible, except for the sand fleas. They were practically invisible and, at night, were quite hungry and delighted to take a bite out of you—a bite that itched as a small, raised bump for days.

We learned to pull our sleeping bags so tightly around us that not one hint of air or fleas could sneak in. Better to be hot and sweaty and longing for morning than to be bitten.

The ocean was divine. Swimming was fun, but also meant you had to be extremely careful of the undertow.

Once in my first Puerto Rican sojourn, I was swimming in the warm ocean and the undertow grew to be especially strong. Luis and friends were on the beach. I found that I couldn't swim against the undertow back to shore. So, for maybe half an hour, I treaded water and went with the waves rocking me back and forth, until finally, a wave washed me close to shore. I was tired, but okay. The guys had been watching me and knew I was all right.

Another clue to go with the flow, and not fight or push against the tide?

And, yes, in our Luquillo tent camp, drugs were a part of the scene. It was the early '70s!

My several trips were with LSD and mushrooms.

One acid trip on the beach at night was particularly intriguing. The moon was full. The air was warm. The water was inviting. At one point, I felt I was seeing large, white, gossamer beings in long, robe-like dress in the sky moving toward Venus. They ascended until they were out of sight.

That stood out for me. I didn't see anything else quite so ethereal.

I was also astounded at the beauty of the sand and the mesmerizing, powerful, magnetic presence of the ocean.

Mushroom ventures meant we had to gather them. We got up before the sun (sun dries out the delicate shrooms), trekked to the Brahma bull fields, and looked for their piles of shit. We had seasoned mushroom spotters with us.

The mushrooms were very small and fragile. We picked some and dropped them into a bag, always keeping a wary eye on the bulls. We needed to be quick at picking. When the bulls saw us, they would charge. We never ventured far from the fences and safety.

Psilocybin journeys were gentle, colorful, and full of good feelings.

Our days on the beach were usually uneventful, but one exciting, triumphal event at the camp occurred when, one afternoon, a police helicopter landed on *our* beach. We were known to the local townspeople, but no one had bothered about us until that day.

Someone had the creative idea for all the women in our band to run out to the helicopter to greet the policemen. Probably eight to ten women clad in long hippie skirts and halter tops ran to the whirlybird, laughing, waving, smiling, and shouting our welcome to the men. The helicopter promptly took off and we never saw them again, at least via helicopter.

Another adventure involved a man who owned a tugboat. He ferried molasses among the Caribbean Islands. He avoided the authorities so he wouldn't have to pay taxes. Somehow, he discovered our camp and showed up one day. He went swimming with us in the ocean and invited a few of us to take a ride on his tugboat. Three or four of us found our way to his boat and went for a ride on the ocean. What a great feeling! It was beautiful. He introduced us to his wife and child. That was their life.

There was a Puerto Rican man from New York City named Michael who was one of our tribe. We called him Mickey. He came to Puerto Rico so he wouldn't be arrested for having marijuana. This was 1972 or '73.

He and I were attracted to each other and became an item.

One evening, Mickey, his friend, and I were walking back to the camp among the trees when we were accosted by three Puerto Rican plainclothes cops. They were not friendly. They insisted that I must know Spanish (I knew very little) and one of them threatened me with a knife, holding it up against my throat. I was strangely serene during that event. Mickey's friend told them calmly in Spanish that I really didn't know Spanish and convinced them that we weren't up to no good.

They let us go.

We went back to our camp and told everyone what had occurred. We surmised that our time was up at that location. That night everyone packed up and got ready to move out the next morning.

It was a stressful night. We didn't sleep.

Laura had connected with Javier, a Puerto Rican man who lived in the middle of the island and owned a mountain there where he grew marijuana. Apparently, he was one of the most wanted criminals in Puerto Rico, but the cops couldn't find him. His family protected him.

Mickey and I decided to go with her to Javier's home.

We hitchhiked and ended up in this magical place in the forest. Javier invited us to try some of his weed. It was the strongest I had ever had, like tripping.

The next morning, Javier wanted to show us the waterfall at the base of his mountain.

That involved a walk down the steep mountain.

Javier was slender, lanky, and playful. He led us like a joyful elf, down the mountain path, bounding lightly from behind one tree in front of us and, somehow or other, ending up walking behind us. He was full of delight.

At the bottom of the mountain were old rock formations with carvings from ancient times. We walked over the massive flat rocks to discover a beautiful waterfall and pool. A few of us laid out on the sun-warmed rocks, soaking up the beauty. Javier dove into the pool.

At one point, he came up from a dive and we locked eyes for a long moment. Then he went down again. I thought he was just playing, like his sprite-like self when he danced around us on the mountain trek downhill.

But he didn't surface. For a few minutes.

I became alarmed. No one else seemed to notice. I went to the edge of the pool and dove in. I found him on the bottom, his body floating in a sitting position with arms extended.

I pulled him up, remembering old life-saving techniques from high school.

I swam with him to the edge. He was limp and unresponsive. I still wondered if he was playing with me.

Mickey saw us and came to help. He was able to drag Javier out of the water and I directed him to lay him flat on his back. He wasn't breathing. I turned his head to the side to try and drain water from his lungs.

I started CPR, alternating with breaths and compressions. More water came out of his lungs. I continued, without success.

During our frolic to the waterfall, Laura had stayed in the house at the top of the mountain. She heard that something was wrong and came down to see. When she saw Javier, she came undone.

Meanwhile, someone went to call the police.

After a while, they came. They relieved me, and I went back up the mountain to the house, along with Mickey and the others.

Here, we were confronted with the family. At some point, he was pronounced dead, and his mother and other women relatives began wailing in grief.

We ascertained that the family blamed us for his death. They were very hostile.

Later, Laura told us that he had a heart condition and we surmised that he had had a heart attack, probably from shooting up with a drug he shouldn't have after our mountain descent.

We realized we just needed to leave. We were in danger. That was when the police took care of us. They loaded four or five of us into the back of their paddy wagon and drove us to another town on the southwest part of the island.

By that time, it was night. They let us off next to a Catholic church.

We had no money and no real idea of where we were.

We knocked on the giant church door with no response. Then we went around to what could have been the rectory (the priests' quarters). A priest opened the door and Mickey, in Spanish, told him we had no place to stay.

The very kind priest let us stay overnight in some rooms behind the church sanctuary. It was a long, sleepless night.

In an adjacent room was a statue of Jesus, prone, with painted blood draining out of the wound in his side. He looked very much like Javier. Laura was overcome with grief again.

The next day, we parted ways with Laura and the others. Mickey knew of a place in the mountains at Mayaguez, a town in the southwest corner of the island, where we could stay.

We hitchhiked and found it. It had probably been erected by traveling hippies. It was a hut with a wood floor, beams supporting a tin roof, and no sides, halfway up a mountain. Down a path nearby was a tree house in a mango tree.

No one was there, so we moved in. Mickey was able to go to the town market below and rustle up some food, thanks to the generosity of local residents. He also went jungle foraging nearby and found bananas, mangos, breadfruit, and other yummy native fruits.

I discovered that I could bake the breadfruit by building a wood fire in the base of an old metal stove that had been left there. We added butter and yum! It wasn't bad.

Some nights, we slept in the mango tree house. Breakfast in the morning entailed reaching over the branch near our wooden bed platform and picking a mango to munch on.

Sometimes we would hike down the mountain—which was steep—and fish for rock lobsters in the stream below. They were very delicious when dipped in butter.

At one point, a man Mickey met in the town gave us a kitten. So sweet. One of my favorite times was evening when the light was dimming, the forest sounds were quieting, and things were becoming more still. That was when our kitten came alive, bounding all around as if she was privy to sounds we couldn't hear. Evening life around us was stirring.

During my month or two at Mayaguez, I read books that had been left in the hut—books by Gurdjieff, and Ouspensky's *The Fourth Way*. The books gave me other ideas about things being more than what they seem to the five senses. I was intrigued and wanted to know more.

We were in the midst of a rainy season. Afternoons, the sky would open up and torrents of rain would pour down on the tin roof, in a continuous volley like a deafening drumroll.

After an hour, it just stopped. The sun came out and the air was beautiful, fresh, and clean.

We were rain barrel savers. We had big metal barrels that we put underneath the downspouts at the corners of the hut to collect rain from the wet sky bursts. One day, I was taking a sponge bath just outside our hut using the water we had collected.

Suddenly, over the crest of the mountain, appeared a semicircle of about eight police.

Mickey, being the diplomatic individual that he was, went up to inquire of them.

It appeared that they had heard that this mountain was a marijuana plantation, and they were coming to bust it. Mickey asked them nicely if his wife (that sounded better than "girlfriend") could get dressed first. They very kindly agreed and didn't come any closer until I had put on clothes.

Then they proceeded to comb the mountain for evidence of the flourishing weed. They found nothing. Mickey and I were glad that the pot seeds he had planted in small containers had never come up!

They left puzzled and probably disappointed, and that was that.

To get Laura, her daughter, and me to Puerto Rico, we needed to fly. I had a little money in the bank, but she had nothing. Her husband kept all his income in order to control her movements.

The school where we were got paid in checks by the parents. The accounting system was sloppy. The checks were left loose in a drawer in a desk in the main office.

Laura convinced me to steal a check and cash it at the local bank so we would have plane fare. I was persuaded, though I had doubts, and stole a check for $250. I took it to the bank and told them I was employed by the school. They cashed it. I must have looked honest. We had all the money we needed for the flight.

One day in our hut in Mayaguez, I got a letter from the postman that was inside an envelope from my parents. It was from the director of the school. They had found out that I had stolen the check and said they would have me arrested. But if I paid it back, they would forget about it.

So, I knew I had to come back to the states and take care of this. I said goodbye to a sad Mickey. I always hoped he did well. He is a good person.

That was around August 1972. My parents sent me plane fare, and I flew to Newark.

Source Walks with You Continually, Presenting Opportunities According to Your Nature

I didn't want to live with my parents. Some of that was guilt, some of it was hiding why I had come back at that time, and some of it was just a feeling that it was time for me to get on with whatever was next.

I thought of Cambridge, Massachusetts, where a few years earlier I had so much enjoyed the summer learning open classroom techniques and throwing pottery on a wheel.

I investigated roommate situations and found an apartment with a few guys who needed a roommate. The price was right, so I moved in.

In high school, I learned to type quite easily, reaching sixty words per minute fairly rapidly. That was probably because I had taken piano lessons from third grade through high school and my hand-eye coordination was decent. With those skills, I was able to get a temp job as a typist.

With the money I earned from that job, I paid back my debt to the school and never heard from them again.

Evan was one of my roommates in Cambridge. Sarah was his girlfriend. She and I hit it off right away. She needed to move to a new apartment and wanted to know if I would be her roommate. I said yes. She also introduced me to Joseph.

Psychedelics Open Up
Your Brain Pathways

The first night I connected to Joseph we dropped acid, probably Purple Haze. The encounter was intense and in a really good way. We were bonded.

Sarah was okay with Joseph moving in with us. Joseph and I became a couple, like fast!

He was very easygoing and smart. He had lived in California and from there had saved a few hits of orange sunshine (acid with mescaline), which he kept in the freezer. He said they were old so probably didn't have much punch.

Uh-uh! Nope. One day we decided to drop some. We thought we'd try a hit and a half because they were so old and probably less potent.

We dropped and took a walk. On the way home. I could barely figure out how to walk—the sidewalk was undulating. Joseph had to practically carry me back.

In the apartment, we lay on the living room floor for maybe an hour where the drug took over our brains, rendering us basically unable to move. I remember being a bit worried, but I also realized that if I surrendered to what was, I would probably be in better shape than if I fought it.

Another clue about letting go of control.

After an hour, we could move again. Then I proceeded to have one of the most loving, expansive experiences I had ever had. I saw rainbows everywhere. My friend Janice came over and she looked incredibly beautiful! I felt fabulous, joyful, and in love with everything. Everything from the plants to the furniture to the food felt alive and part of a whole living, connected energy.

The trip lasted maybe eight to ten hours. Then we slept it off. I wouldn't do it today. It takes a toll on your system. But it gave me a taste of joy and love—felt physically, emotionally, and mentally— that was replicated in later years through meditation and spiritual experiences, but without the physical toll.

Without knowing it, I was on a path into the Divine.

Meditation: Humility and Our True Self

"By God, when you see your beauty, you will be the idol of yourself." —Rumi

The amount of humility we have is directly proportionate to the degree of spiritual connection and blessings we can have and give.

The love of Spirit for you is behind it all.

You are loved beyond your knowing, without end.

Let Creation love you.

True humility is seeing your own magnificence.

Humility is an elusive thing. When you think of humility, what do you think of?

Not fawning or groveling, but true humility.

As I meditate and sink more deeply into the arms of the Infinite, I feel more and more subtle layers of tension relaxing and letting go.

I experience perhaps the beginnings of humility as Spirit pruning, dissolving the layers of my ego and my resistance, both conscious and unconscious.

I am aware that I need to do nothing, fear nothing; just relax, trust, and receive. Receive my Self, as part of the Whole of Divinity.

There is no need to construct an ego or a false self to present to the world.

I already am a Self, wholly loved, wholly Whole and magnificent. I came this way.

And so did You.

I loved Cambridge. I loved Charles River, MIT, and the beautiful Harvard campus. It had a small town feel then—coffee houses with guitar gigs, parks, and Fresh Pond, a small lake where joggers and bikers can circle round for exercise.

And as I write this, I notice that Cambridge appears in my history: River Cam in Cambridge, England; attraction to Pembroke College (originally in Cambridge, England) in Rhode Island; and now, Cambridge, Massachusetts. I draw no conclusion; just noticing.

Work at that time consisted of temporary typing jobs until I landed a job being an aide at Fernald School in Waltham, Massachusetts. Now, in researching this school, I am horrified and my heart hurts.

The Fernald Center was originally called the Experimental School for Teaching and Training Idiotic Children. It was founded in Boston in 1848.

At its peak, 2,500 kids were housed there, most of them so-called "feeble-minded" boys.

Its third superintendent was Walter Fernald (1859–1924). He was an advocate of eugenics. The school was viewed as a model educational facility in the field of what was then called mental retardation. It was renamed in his honor in 1925.

The institution served a large population of children with cognitive disabilities. At the time, they were called "mentally retarded children," but, "Massachusetts officials acknowledged that in 1949, …about 8 percent of children in state schools were not mentally retarded or were normal." (Allen 2004)

Living conditions were awful. About thirty-six children slept in each dormitory room. There were also reports of physical and sexual abuse.

Fernald used the residents in sterilization and radiation experiments.

From 1946 to 1953, joint experiments by Harvard and MIT exposed young male children to tracer doses of radioactive isotopes.

- The experiment was conducted in part by a research grant from Quaker Oats Company.
- MIT Professor of Nutrition Robert S. Harris led the experiment, which studied the absorption of calcium and iron.
- The boys were encouraged to join a so-called "Science Club," which offered larger portions of food, parties, and trips to Boston Red Sox baseball games.
- The fifty-seven club members ate iron-enriched cereals and calcium-enriched milk for breakfast. To track absorption, several radioactive calcium tracers were given orally or intravenously.
- Researchers measured radiation levels in stool and blood samples

- In another study, children received iron supplement shots containing radioisotopes of iron.
- Neither the children nor their parents were ever given adequate informed consent for participation in a scientific study.

According to *Smithsonian Magazine*, "The Fernald students' experiment was just one among dozens of radiation experiments approved by the Atomic Energy Commission." (Boissoneault 2017)

This scene changed in the 1970s, when a class action suit, *Ricci v. Okin*, was filed to upgrade conditions at Fernald and several other state institutions for persons with so-called "mental retardation" in Massachusetts.

U.S. District Court Judge Joseph Louis Tauro, in 1993, said that improvements in the care and conditions at the school had made them "second to none anywhere in the world." (Tauro 1993)

A 1995 class-action suit resulted in a 1998 district court decision awarded the "group of former students who ate radioactive oatmeal as unwitting participants in a food experiment ... share(d) a $1.85 million settlement from Quaker Oats and the Massachusetts Institute of Technology." (The Associated Press 1998)

I include this very disturbing information only to show the huge divide between those who come from a place of love and consider the dignity and sovereignty of the people they are serving, and those who come from a position of complete disconnection from and disregard for their subjects. Love doesn't abuse.

It could be that when I went to work there in 1972 or '73, this class action suit was in play. I hope so.

I was a nurse's aide. We bathed, fed, and played with the developmentally disabled kids.

I remember one young lady (I think she was a teenager) who lived in a crib. She had hydrocephalus (accumulation of a lot of fluid in the head) and her body was small.

Her bones had not grown very much, and they were gnarly. Her head was very large and so heavy that when I lifted her head one day to wash her, I was afraid I would drop her. Thankfully, I didn't.

One young man stands out for me. Mark was about eleven years old, small, developmentally disabled, blind, and deaf. There was no attempt by the school to work with him. I very much wanted to connect with him somehow.

One day I took him to the bathroom. As he sat in his stall and I waited outside, I started tapping on the outside of the metal stall.

He felt it and became alert. I tapped again with a rhythm. He felt it, his eyes lit up and he started laughing.

He tried to duplicate the tapping. I almost cried. We sat that way, tapping back and forth for a while. Whenever I worked with him again, we tapped. We made a human connection.

Now I work with clients using EFT—the Tapping Solution. It's not exactly the same, but I like the parallel of rhythmic tapping that creates healing. Something deep inside our bodies responds.

Meditation

Allow yourself to feel the rhythm of the universe. What would that be? The rhythm of the seasons. The cycle of the spinning Earth revolving around the sun and the moon orbiting Earth. Rhythm. Movement in response to rhythm.

The rhythm of wings. Hummingbirds. Sparrows. Eagles. Movement in relation to air, energy.

Motivation, force, will, intent directing the beat of your heart. Rhythm. Body functions, breathing. Rhythm.

Cycles of the moon. Rhythm. Five elements in sync—air, water, fire, earth, and cosmic ether in rhythm. Wheels of the bus go 'round and 'round. Rhythm.

What is your rhythm? All harmonious. All notes in the grand symphony of life, creation. We are the instruments of the chorus, the orchestra. We play our notes. What note, what tune will you play? Sometimes dissonance happens. But:

"If we understood the world, we would realize that there is a logic of harmony underlying its manifold apparent dissonances." — Jean Sibelius (Thomas & Thomas 1946, 309)

Cambridge Light Explorations

My Cambridge roommate, Sarah, was a healer. She was very intuitive and used the energy coming through her hands to help people heal.

She set up a retreat for folks to develop their intuition. I went. I had never done anything like that before. She led us through exercises in visualization and I found it quite easy.

We were well taken care of by the hostess, who served us delicious meals that felt unbelievably nourishing.

Toward the end of our uplifting couple of days, I went outside into the woods. It was raining lightly, and I felt like I was being baptized.

This, for me, was a formalized beginning into expanding my intuition and trusting what sounds and images appeared in my inner awareness.

The following meditation came from my listening. As I sat in meditation, the inner voice urged, "Get up and write."

Meditation: Stay Tuned to Your Inner Voice

I have done so, continuing to listen. As I type the words, I allow my body, mind, and heart to respond to their invitations. I am meditating with you as you respond to the promptings.

As I write, I am learning what this book will be about. I am in an active discovery. It is exciting! I love exploring and discovering. We will explore together. That is the best fun! We are companions on our journey together!

I don't know what is next. But that's all the fun! The surprise.

I am not concerned because I trust that Spirit is guiding me. It is like opening presents on Christmas morning. You know it's going to be something awesome when they are from someone who loves you, delights in your delight, and wants you to be joyful.

I am joyful writing these words because I also anticipate that we will grow together. We will not be the same persons at the completion of these words if we have allowed the essence, the soul of this lyric to touch our own foundation, be it physical, mental, emotional, or spiritual.

And, as with all creative compositions, I invite you to stay tuned to your own inner voice while engaging in my content.

When you notice an itch or discord inside, in your head or heart or body, pause. Pay attention. What doesn't feel right to you? Sit with yourself and your itch. What is it telling you? These inner proddings are there to align you with yourself. How do you feel? What is truth to you in this moment?

There are many ways to the Divine. Returning to my time in Cambridge, MA, Sarah also knew a few men who were exploring spirituality and sound. I was introduced to a beautiful twenty-minute sound piece that brought me to another feeling of calm—physically, mentally, and emotionally. I felt expansive and energized.

Over the years, I have found many beautiful healing sound pieces that effect change in a person, from relieving pain to creating peace or promoting energy and joy. These I have used with myself and my clients to help us come back into balance.

I was also shown how to access past lives through a meditation practice. I explored a number of what appeared to be past lives. The idea was to help heal whatever wounds had been received during those times. Whether or not these were actually past lives didn't matter. I knew that the visuals and events came out of my unconscious, so whatever the cause, the act of healing the pain was good.

Joseph and I moved to a house shared with four or five other folks near Fresh Pond in Cambridge. We had a room upstairs. I hung a spider plant in our large window. It grew huge. We had a multicolored cat Joseph called Frothing Slosh.

Charlie lived there with his little black dog, Malinowski. Malinowski was amazing (probably like the Polish anthropologist). He would get on the streetcar by himself to ride downtown and go for a walk. When his walk was complete, he would jump back on the streetcar and come home. The streetcar drivers knew him and were happy to give him a ride, free of charge!

One of the books I read at that time was *The Aquarian Gospel of Jesus the Christ*. It affected me deeply.

One afternoon, I was sitting outside in our backyard eating my rice for lunch. Suddenly, I was overcome by a strong, beneficent force. I couldn't eat. All I could do was sit with it.

In my mind's eye, I saw Jesus sitting at the end of a long table. On either side of the table were other spiritual teachers who were working with and for him.

He was talking to me. At one point he reached out and touched my forehead.

The powerful energy lasted maybe 20-30 minutes. It felt like an invitation to keep walking the spiritual path. I had no idea what would occur later.

Following the Inner Nudge

About two years into my three years in Cambridge, I had the idea to move to Northern California. There was no discernible, concrete reason; I just had a feeling. At first, I thought it was interesting, but then the feeling stayed and stayed.

After two years with Joseph, I was beginning to feel differently about him. He was depressed and not doing anything about it. It was affecting me. I felt heavy being with him. Our initial fun, interesting life together had lapsed.

I moved to an apartment with Sarah, my healer friend.

With Sarah, I began to explore my own desire to help people feel better. She and I took a basic acupressure class. I use that knowledge today.

I also took classes in basic Swedish massage and other modalities. I got work in health clubs doing massage for the clients.

Sarah and I also decided we would try to create our own healing business. We set up one room in our apartment as our healing room.

We weren't super successful. She was more than I.

I had one male client who, like some, wanted more than a therapeutic massage. That was a *nope* and I ushered him out.

But my time in Cambridge, especially with Sarah, led me to explore and experience spirituality—life beyond the five senses and healing work that I could do that incorporated my growing belief that body, mind, and spirit had to align for real healing to occur.

Sarah was also a devotee of Swami Muktananda, an Indian Guru. She introduced me to his style of spirituality with chanting and Siddhi yoga. I didn't realize that this was a precursor to some of my next adventures.

My feeling to move to California persisted. I decided to move, to follow this persistent feeling. I began to make plans.

At that time, we were living in Somerville, MA, a town adjacent to Cambridge.

One day, I was having lunch by myself in the grassy park next to the Charles River. A young man, Daniel, saw me and came over to chat. We had a nice conversation and decided to stay connected.

Over time, Daniel discovered that I needed an apartment for a few months before going through with my plans to move to California. He said that across the street from him a young woman was looking for a roommate. He introduced us and I had a place to rent until December 1975.

Daniel and I started hanging out. Turned out he loved to cook and was into making very healthy meals. That was fun and delicious.

We got along and went on weekend trips together. The last weekend before my journey to the west, we went to a small-town B&B on the coast of Maine during a full moon. Magical.

After making love, I was filled with so much energy I couldn't sleep. I got up at midnight and walked to the sea edge. My body was electrified; surges of energy charged through me for over an hour. I felt like I was one with the energy of the sea.

Daniel and I knew we were short-term. I said goodbye in late December of 1975 and landed in San Francisco around Christmastime.

I have never moved from the west coast.

California Love—Deeper into the Heart of Source

My beautiful sister, Liza, was living in San Francisco at that time in an apartment in the Noe Valley district on Army Street (since renamed Cesar Chavez St). She let me camp on her floor for a week.

I remember going to Golden Gate Park during my first few days on the west coast. There were tiny white flowers growing in the grass. I loved those little flowers. I felt welcomed and that I had made the right decision to move west.

In that first week, I found myself interested in the Sivananda Yoga Center in the Sunset district. I had really liked my hatha yoga classes in Stamford, CT, and found that there were more yoga centers in SF.

One information flyer for them advertised that a yogi named Sant Keshavadas, known as the Singing Saint, was going to be doing an evening of kirtan at their center. (Kirtan, from a Sanskrit root meaning "to cut through," is what musician David Newman calls "a practice for cutting through the idea of separation, for connecting to our hearts and connecting to the moment through sound." (Kripalu Center)

I was curious and decided to attend.

He was an engaging fellow who played the harmonium and sang many chants in Sanskrit, an ancient language of India. I believe he did a brief talk on Bhakti Yoga.

According to Alyssa Hullett of Greatist, "Bhakti's all about breaking down barriers. Breaking barriers to love, to other people, to the Divine, and to the interconnectedness of all things. This can help you experience the beauty and love of the moment." (Hullett 2021)

The evening was very moving for me. I felt strong loving energy not unlike the energy I felt when Jesus touched my forehead in Cambridge.

After the event, I went up to Sant to say thank you. I didn't get to utter a word when he saw me and said, "I recognize you. I invite you to join me, if you like, in my events. I will call you Ananda."

I had no idea what Ananda meant (I found out later it means "joy, bliss, fullness, and happiness") but I thought it might be interesting to see what he was up to.

Thus began a two-year adventure with the Singing Saint.

I knew I couldn't crash on my sister's floor forever. I needed an apartment.

Another guy, Jacob, who liked what Sant Keshavadas was teaching and loved the spiritual energy he manifested, needed an apartment also. Sant invited the two of us to become a center for him in San Francisco. Since he traveled a lot, he hadn't put down too many roots, in terms of home bases. He had one main one in Virginia Beach.

We thought, *Why not?* We found a three-bedroom place in the sunset district, on 21st and Judah. It was a pink house with maybe seven or eight steps going up to the front door.

Jacob loved the energy that Santji, as Sant was also called, helped to manifest. He would really vibe to it, smiling, laughing, in joy.

I had a crush on Jacob. It went no further than that.

We did become a little center. We planned Sant's events when he came into town. We held meditations and pujas at our home.

The word "puja" is Sanskrit and means reverence, honor, homage, adoration, and worship. Puja, the loving offering of light, flowers, and water or food to the Divine, is an essential ritual of Hinduism.

When I performed the pujas, especially when doing the chanting (from the Sanskrit prayers), once again, I felt very strong, loving energy throughout my body, mind, and feelings.

We explored the different deities of Hinduism: Saraswati, Durga, Shiva, and Krishna, for instance.

Santji said one of my guides was Saraswati. She is the Hindu goddess of knowledge, music, art, speech, wisdom, and learning. She is a part of the trinity of Saraswati, Lakshmi, and Parvati.

Lakshmi is the Hindu goddess of wealth, good fortune, youth, and beauty. She is the wife of the god Vishnu.

Parvati is the Hindu goddess of fertility, love, beauty, harmony, marriage, children, and devotion, as well as of divine strength and power.

I meditated on Saraswati and the attributes of her qualities.

I was never much into the guru idea where you devote yourself to another person and Sant was cool with that. He did have some devotees who were all in with that style and he honored and understood that road to Spirit.

The title of his movement was "Temple of Cosmic Religion." He often propounded that "Truth is One. Many are the Names." That sat well with me.

His events were colored with music—he played the harmonium and channeled song from Spirit. People loved the energy he created.

He was on a mission to unite all world religions in one religion of love, a mission that led him to travel globally, meeting with such spiritual leaders as Mother Teresa and Pope Paul VI. He taught that "Love born of wisdom can solve all problems," and, "Truth is one; many are the names. God is one; paths are many." Speaking eight languages, he sought to bring together East and West, ancient and modern, and wrote more than 50 books and 6,000 kirtans.

I spent two years learning and growing with Sant in the late 1970s and I feel he has influenced my life profoundly in many ways, then and since. As I reflect on this beautiful soul, my heart is humbled. I'm tearing up in gratitude for how he helped me on my spiritual and life path.

At one point, he said to me that I was transparent, meaning, I believe, that I was open to receiving the Divine. He was right.

He was very personable. He could see how each of us was needing to grow and facilitated our movement in that direction.

When I first hung out with him, I found out I was pregnant, from that magical time with Daniel in Maine. I felt completely unprepared to bring a child into the world.

I had a temp job and made very little money. I couldn't imagine how I would raise a child and work. I couldn't envision myself even being a mom and felt I would be bad at it. I was ashamed and scared.

Santji understood and, without judgment, supported me in doing whatever I needed to. I got an abortion at UCSF.

Afterward, I grieved, wrote letters to my pregnancy, held little ceremonies to engage with my pregnancy, and with time, healed. I understand the me I was then. There is no judgment. I understand women in similar or more difficult circumstances.

Many years later, my Indian son, whom we adopted, was born on July 15, 1997. Santji died on December 4, 1997, at sixty-three years of age.

I have felt and wondered if Santji was instrumental in helping me come full circle around to being a mother this lifetime. And did he help me heal from that long ago pain?

After a time of hanging out with Sant Keshavadas, I started getting a feeling that I wasn't growing. I had a dream about him that seemed to help separate me from that type of energy.

I told him I was moving on. He was okay and just said, "Don't think ill of me." I really didn't. I think I was just done with that section of life.

Arizona Light—
The Pull of Nature

My friend Janice, from Boston, had moved into our San Francisco apartment.

She and I met in the back of a Volkswagen van around 1973 or '74 when we were going to New Jersey for Thanksgiving to see our respective families. She was living in Boston; I, in Cambridge.

Her apartment was several feet from an elevated train. I could never for the life of me understand how she could deal with the thundering clamor of the train going by. But she did.

We hit it off and stayed in touch. When she decided to come west, I told her she could rent a room in our apartment.

Janice and I had some good adventures!

With a couple of guys one summer, we went to Mount Shasta. We hiked up the mountain and camped. We soaked in the hot springs nearby and absorbed the energy of the mountain.

Another time—I can't remember why—we hitchhiked to Arizona. Probably it was the pull of Indian Hot Springs near the southeastern border of New Mexico. We went by way of Bisbee, a mile-high, small former copper mining desert community laid out mostly on a mountainside, one hundred miles southeast of Tucson.

Bisbee held good vibes for us.

We met like-minded people and vowed to return after our hot springs soak.

The part of the hot springs expedition I remember most is the mud soak. We smeared warm hot springs mud all over our bodies and laid out in the sun, letting the mud bake and evict toxins from our bodies, minds, and spirits. Then we washed off in the hot mineral stream and swam in the cool pool. Remembering that makes me want to do it right now!

I loved the desert! To me, there was nothing else like it.

The deep, powerful earth energy spoke to me and electrified my body and spirit. In the desert, I felt more alive and connected to myself in ways I never had before.

I loved the rocks. They too were more alive to me than I had sensed anywhere else.

After the hot springs jaunt, Janice and I hitchhiked back through Bisbee. We had a feeling of home there. We met people who welcomed us. They were folks like us—hippie types, artists, and musicians. We decided we would get our stuff in California and come back to live there.

22

More Spiritual Excursions

Bisbee provided me with other explorations of my spiritual life—what I could give to others and what the desert could give to me.

This little mile-high desert town had been a copper, gold, and silver mining center, called "Queen of the Copper Camps."

Janice and I felt at home there.

There was a plethora of minerals—copper derivatives, among others, such as azurite, malachite, chrysocolla, and more—with which artists made jewelry to sell. Janice became a talented jewelry creator and sold some of her work in the Copper Queen Hotel.

Bisbee had a co-op, which added to our feeling right at home. To make some money, we learned how to make tofu and sold it to the co-op.

Thomas, the juicer, was a local icon. He made all kinds of wonderful fresh juice at the co-op. He and Janice had a thing.

One house we rented was on the south side of the mountain. The compact houses were scrunched together, and all sounds echoed off the canyon walls, so you heard everything! Many sleepless nights were caused by the seemingly all-night barking of dogs. One dog would start and then the chorus would ensue.

A Regular Job With Challenges

I knew I had to make more money than was manifesting from tofu-making.

I applied to and was hired to work at a home for disabled adults. It was about three miles southeast of town. I had no car, so a bike had to do.

I worked the afternoon/evening shift, getting off at 11 p.m.

Going to work was easy. I would ride out of town past the Lavender Pit Mine (all downhill), over old railroad tracks, through a neighborhood (might have been Warren), past barking, aggressive dogs (I learned to carry rocks to throw at them as they tried to bite my ankles. Yelling only made them more determined.), and finally to the house for disabled men.

Coming home at night was challenging because of the mile-high uphill climb into town. And some nights, when I was tired, I wished the hill were not quite so steep. I gained a lot of leg muscle strength during those months.

In this home, we were supposed to help these men learn basic skills: cooking, cleaning, and such. We also took them on outings in the house van to interesting places.

I remember three of the guys. One was Fred. He was Mexican, about fifty or sixty years old, and he laughed a lot. He enjoyed calling me crazy when I teased him ("Ann, chou crazy!") and would laugh at my weirdness.

Another guy was younger and had grand mal seizures. He wore a football helmet because he kept hitting his head when he would seize. At first, it was a bit scary, but I learned to put a bite stick in between his teeth to keep him from biting his tongue and put pillows around him so he wouldn't hurt himself. Being able to help him with the inevitable eased my tension a bit.

Another guy (I'll call him James) was big—maybe six feet, three inches—and heavy. He was prone to anger outbursts where he would growl and rock back and forth and rage and want to do damage. He couldn't control it; it just came on unpredictably from some undefined trigger. He scared the other men. They usually read the signs and exited the room.

We were supposed to keep everyone safe, but we were not trained for managing this behavior! (Later, in another job, I learned how to deal with people in rage events.)

It seemed like he had a buildup of tension and had not learned any other option to release it. After a bit of raging, thankfully, he would calm down and so would we.

Once, I drove the van on an outing with four or five of the men. James was in the back. I heard the familiar growl and, looking in the rear-view mirror, saw him rocking back and forth. I knew that this would not turn out well; he was contained in a small space and couldn't move about to relieve his energy

Not knowing exactly what to do, I stopped the van on the side of the road and told him to get out and walk it off. I didn't know if this would work or if he would get more out of control and worse things would happen.

But he did what I said and after maybe twenty minutes, he calmed down. I seem to remember that when I gave him a very strong verbal directive, he listened.

Now from my therapy training, I can guess that he felt out of control and had never been given the tools to deal with whatever was going on inside.

Or perhaps he had never had boundaries that were meant to keep him safe. I wonder if he had been abused or hurt in some way and if something or other in the day would trigger the pain, which made him mad.

He did what so many do when pain is felt—he got angry. Anger gives a person a sense of power, whereas pain makes people feel vulnerable and powerless. Most people reject or even hate feeling powerless.

I had never dealt with anger before (except once in college). Anger was verboten in my house growing up. My dad disdained it, so we three kids stuffed our anger.

When I first got to college, one day I was in my dorm room with my two roommates. I was sitting on a bed next to one. The other was on the bed opposite.

The one sitting next to me was verbally railing against the other one. She was going after her pretty nastily, I thought. I wasn't liking this at all. Without thinking or even knowing what I was doing, my left arm, as if with a mind of its own, struck out sideways and smacked her in the stomach knocking the wind out of her.

They were surprised. I was surprised. But I guess I accomplished my goal. She quit berating my other roommate.

I was being a lot like James. I was unaware of my anger. My body was, however, and acted on its own.

When I was home on vacation from college that fall, I confronted my parents about not dealing with anger in our house. They walked out of the room. I supposed this was something I would have to deal with myself.

My life would take me down other paths that would teach me to deal with anger—to understand it and how suppressing it may lead to depression, physical ailments, and other consequences.

When I decided to leave the Bisbee job, I wrote a long note to the employer (I think it was Cochise County) saying that their lack of employee training to deal with aggressive clients was endangering the employees and the clients and I hoped they would rethink their policy and put the safety of all first. I have no idea if they ever did.

Exploring Energy and Healing Through Nature

Bisbee was high desert. It got hot, but not as hot as Tucson or Phoenix. We lived with scorpions. We had to shake out our shoes and pants to make especially sure that the smaller, more poisonous white scorpions were not hiding in there.

Rattlesnakes are part of the desert. But in my whole time in Bisbee, I never encountered one, even though I traipsed around the desert regularly and one day in bare feet!

Peyote was also available. A couple of times, I decided with friends to take a peyote journey. My mushroom adventures in Puerto Rico had made me curious about it and I figured that with care and honor of the spirit of the cactus, we would be okay.

We had fresh buttons and dried buttons. Since we knew that ingesting the buttons leads to nausea and often vomiting, we got creative.

Someone invented a smoothie that also included fruit so it didn't taste as bitter as the herb. Another style that bypassed the digestive tract was to blend the plant with warm water and then you were ready for your peyote enema.

The journey I remember occurred one day when I ate eight fresh buttons. By some digestive miracle, I was able to keep them all inside my body.

We had decided to make this experience as respectful and sacred as we could. We built a circle of stones where we invited in the consciousness of peyote and all those unseen protective spiritual beings who would want to help us on our travels. We would begin our adventure in this circle. As I write this, I can still feel the support of the peyote spirit.

I don't recall a lot about this encounter except that I felt wonderful, protected, expansive, and connected to the desert—to the rocks, the chayote, and the cacti. That was the time I tripped around the desert in bare feet, with nary a sting or prick or bite to jab me.

After leaving the style of spirituality of Bhakti Yoga and Sant, I became interested in healing modalities, a continuation of my massage, energy, and intuitive studies from Cambridge.

In Bisbee, I experimented with holding intuition and healing classes where I would lead folks through an exercise to grow their intuition and practice intentional healing through laying on of hands. My friend, Janice, complained that she could feel me inside her head, and it was too strong! I didn't know my own strength and I had to tone myself down and learn to modulate.

I learned about crystals and their properties. In our classes, we would gather different crystals, such as quartz, amethyst, azurite, malachite, and chrysocolla, then lie down and put one on top of each of our chakras to clear and energize them. There are seven main chakras, the blockage of which can cause imbalance in the mind, emotions, or body. The word "chakra," according to *Yoga Journal*, means "spinning wheel." Chakras are "thought to be spinning disks of energy that should stay 'open' for optimal emotional and physical well-being." (Ferretti 2021)

I met other folks who were exploring their spiritual life. Some were quite intuitive. One guy told me that our spiritual learning styles were alike: we took our time, one foot in front of the other, slowly growing in Spirit. I don't know if he was right, but at the time I took in and considered what he said.

He introduced me to an Italian tenor (I forget which one) whom he felt was channeling Spirit through his singing. As I listened to him, I felt a profound depth of emotion that stirred my heart and brought tears to my eyes.

Over the years, I would study sound and its effects on the body, mind, and spirit. And I would seek out musicians who learned how to help people heal through their voices or instruments.

I read books written by other spiritual seekers and tried some of their styles. As I persisted in talking in my head to certain spiritual beings I was drawn to, I found that I was able to *hear* their responses to me in varying ways.

Sometimes I heard small voices in my head that gave me a word or phrase that was appropriate to my question.

Or I would have a felt sense—my body would feel differently: I'd have more energy, feel calmer, have a sense of being loved, a sense of someone close and caring, or a desire to take care of myself somehow (drinking water or eating an apple, for instance).

Or my eye would be drawn to a picture that was relevant to what my question had been. Or a song would appear in my head that was an answer.

I learned and grew to trust that we have an enormous amount of help in the Divine realms. We are not alone. We are cared for, even if we don't know it.

And I also discovered that a Divine Being will not force themself on us—no coercion, no control. They wait for our invitation and, with great respect for our free will, let us take the initiative with them.

I found that when we open the door, even just a little bit, they will respond with Love in its infinite forms in the most appropriate way for what we need.

Time out for a meditation.

Meditation: 10-7-2020 "Divine Mother"

I enter meditation and am surrounded by a very expansive, loving energy. She introduces herself as Divine Mother.

I am invited to sit with her as a friend, to draw and play, to be in joy. We are like two children, skipping, jumping, and laughing in the quantum field of infinite possibilities.

25

Intertwining Linear and Quantum Life and Light

To return to the very beginning of my story.

I asked Theos (remember the community of Streams of Divine Consciousness?) for help since I had been tasked to listen to the recording, but I couldn't access it. I had emailed and messaged the group to get help. It wasn't to be.

What I did hear when I asked Theos was giggling. My sense was that they were telling me that there are always detours. And isn't it useful to laugh at the incongruity and adjust to what is in the moment? (Shades of Janice and my sailing "win" in college when we let go and enjoyed the ride.)

So, since I didn't have the recording, I adjusted. At night before bed, I asked Theos if they could take me to the quantum field, the place of creation, of infinite possibilities and probabilities, while I slept.

That night, I had a dream that I walked from Maine to California in a couple of hours. And in the dream, it was no big deal. I just nonchalantly walked 3,000 miles in two hours. And got to enjoy all the sights along the way.

Still dreaming, I stopped in California and was planning to walk through Oregon and Washington, stopping the night at a hotel because it was cold. Then I woke up.

In a different mindset other than our normal Beta—our brainwave state when we're awake, talking, and thinking—walking across the country in a couple of hours is completely possible. (Check out brainwave states like alpha, beta, and delta at: https://nhahealth. com/brainwaves-the-language/.) It happens when we access the quantum field (you can use other names, like All That Is, Source) through meditation.

Before I got my AIC to begin this tome, I got curious about what was going on at the time of my birth. I found that the weather was mild, and the moon was waning.

I found some information about people and events on my birthday.

But the most fun info for me was that since I was born, I have slept twenty-four years. I've been alive for over 26,000 days. That's about 630,000 hours or almost 37,000,000 minutes.

That's a bit. Time to write my book.

To my conscious knowledge my curiosity about what is real and how we experience this started when I was fifteen. It has continued ever since.

How do we have an experience of what the religious mystics talked about: the wholly Other? How do we experience something outside the discernment of the five senses?

(You can find some definitions on this subject if you like by reading William James, W.T. Stace, Walter Pahnke, David Lukoff, or D.T. Suzuki, to name a few.)

My meditations have gifted me with many delicious feelings, images, and perceptions of Something Other than our normal sensibility of everyday life. These are accompanied by physical, mental, and emotional peace, love, and joy.

Sometimes I am inspired to write about these perceptions.

When I am in a meditation and feel the urge to get up and go to the computer to type, I am usually in a semi-meditative state.

Sometimes my eyes are closed. I don't think or try to come up with words; I just type. (I thank my ten years of piano lessons as a kid and the ease with which I learned to type for facilitating this process.)

So, just as a reminder:

You will continue to discover meditation quotes sprinkled throughout this writing. When you come across them, I invite you to take a few deep breaths and settle into your body. Allow yourself to relax and see if you can let the words move through you as a gentle wave of Light.

Let the words trigger your own connection to Source and see if you can let go of your inclination to try and intellectually understand. (Though if that happens, let it be.) These words came from a place in me when I was letting go, feeling peaceful and energized physically, mentally, and emotionally.

These quotes are not coming from a linear mindset.

Sometimes my psychological understanding mixes in.

If they don't speak to you, no matter. We are all different and we all respond to different styles.

Meditation: 11-16-2020 "On Attachment"

Amazing grace. Buddha. Attachment. Attached to thoughts, feelings, habits, visuals, reactions, things, people. Attachment psychology. Letting go of attachment to reveal yourself and stillness. Divinity.

Meditation Notes: 1-28-2019 "Source and Attachment"

Source coming to me and saying, "Let's take a walk." The walk morphed into "Sit on My Lap." It's about attachment.

In psychology, we talk about secure attachment in a family and the dilemmas with that over the generations.

Often it is a mother wound. Somewhere along the line, a mother may disconnect from her child and her child feels

---

lost, feels the pain of disconnection, feels scared, feels their vulnerability, knows deeply that they cannot survive without the mother or father connection.

They are in a place (Earth) that requires familiarity and perspective and experience with how to negotiate the environment. They need someone who is mature enough to make healthy decisions for them. They need someone with a heart that loves them and so is motivated to give them what they need to grow up healthily.

Source has been saying to me over the years, first, "You are Mine," which brought me a sense of peace, of safety, of being claimed at my core. And, because I felt so much love and safety in that experience, it motivated me to pursue my spiritual journey more intensely, to have more connection with Source, and to explore what relationship is on many levels.

And in other meditations, Source also said to me, "Surrender to Me," which made me say back, "Cool. I'd like to, but I don't really know how to do that. You'll have to help me with that too!"

And noticing that, since asking for help in surrender, which requires trust at a very core level, Spirit has been helping me bit by bit to let go of my anxiety around trust.

My difficulty with trusting others grew out of my early life experience. Possibly at birth, I disconnected from caregivers due to the scene at the time. And, because it was my nature, I became extremely motivated to take care of myself. My parents marveled at their amazing four-month-old feeding herself with a spoon. (I have a different take on "amazing" now. Probably, I was trying to disconnect from something about being fed that didn't feel good.)

In Abraham Maslow's hierarchy of human development, the first job of an infant is learning trust. Then, when that is successfully attained, the next task, and the next, build on the trust and make each subsequent task much easier and more complete.

So not trusting my caregivers led me into a constant core feeling of unconscious mistrust. That sometimes subtle, sometimes flagrant feeling informed my decisions, my emotions, my mind, my behavior, and my choices as I grew up.

Sometimes I just avoided relationships. Sometimes I went to the other extreme, when I was strongly feeling my unmet need for connection and chose relationships that were superficial and not in my best interest.

Of course, it's always a good idea to discern whether others are in it for themselves or have enough self-love to maintain their identity and have plenty of love to give you.

But overall, not growing "trust" from the get-go bounced me very strongly to the other side, to "independence." Not a balanced place, for sure. Either extreme, too much dependence or too much independence, doesn't make for a well-rounded life.

All the while, I had a basic core need to be claimed, to belong, to trust that there was someone capable who had my best interest in mind and had the capacity to provide that when I was vulnerable and not able to negotiate this world by myself.

So, Source said, "Sit on My Lap." So, I did. I had a question, and Source answered it, "I don't have a penis."

So, I sat, and time passed.

And in that space, I could feel a softening of my guard, of my defenses. I relaxed more. As I relaxed more, I felt more love.

And then I heard, "You are Mine."

That was the clincher.

I felt it. I was claimed. I belonged. And I could feel how this time the message rested even more deeply in my Being.

I questioned the sense that Source felt so masculine right then. And then Divine Mother with Her rose-pink essence showed up.

For some reason, Source needed me to feel Him/Her (beyond gender) as masculine first today.

Perhaps it has to do with security, safety, and protection.

And then I asked, "Wouldn't it be more efficient for folks to heal their attachment wounds if You showed up directly? Then all the intergenerational and other disconnections that healers might focus on could be healed right away."

And the reply was, "It will come through you and others and your connection to Me, because We feel your hearts and your compassion, and we will manifest through your surrender to Me."

And so, I will make time to be in relationship with Source and continue to surrender, bit by bit, to All That Is so I may aid others to feel claimed, belonging, adored, and worthy of existence.

Each time I feel more connected to Source, I am motivated to connect even more. The Benefits outweigh the risks!!

Blessings and love for you!

Meditation: 11-17-2020

Buddhas connecting to me. Talking about this book.

Having a relationship with Light. A conversation. Like with a dear old friend.

Letting Light in. Feeling each cell welcoming Light, excited to bond, to be embraced by Light. Allowing Light to cherish every single one of the 30 trillion cells. (Pause a moment and see if you can allow this in yourself.)

In the cherishing, each cell is loved and reaches toward and embraces the Light. In the embrace, a union happens. Energy uplifts.

Joy of each cell as it expands in energy. And each cell recognizes, with increasing awareness, that its sister cells are also expanding in the deliciousness of the Light.

The cells join their energies in one great swell of triumphant, humble merging on the journey of becoming one whole Light Being. The cells know. They have consciousness. They respond to Love.

This is Love in action. This is the Truth of who we are. Our cells are wise. They are simply waiting for the rest of us to realize what actually works.

Love works. Light works. In the Name of All That Is, I proclaim Love as the winner.

In all things be Grateful and all will be added unto you.

Surrendering to the Light is joy-filled, is our birthright. Is our destiny. It's just a matter of when we decide. And by which method. All methods lead to Source. The Grand Master Planner. There is nothing to fear because Source has got this!

We can allow our ego, the need to control out of fear, to rest and take a backseat.

We can learn to trust the Source of Creation, the energy that is really in charge.

Let the blessings rain down on you. Let your spirit soar with Love, with Light. Let all things be subsumed in the purity of Light. This is not a Christian thing. It is not a Buddhist thing. This is a purely Light/Love thing.

Jesus, Buddha, Zoroaster, Mohammed all work together on the inner planes. They don't fight or argue or say, "I know best." They are bonded in Light. They come from the same place.

They were put here on earth to appeal to certain genetic codes and guide the chemical, mathematical codes to the one True location. To the Source of All.

Jesus is love. Mohammed is surrender and love. Buddha is non-attachment and compassion. How can you argue with that?

We must go beyond the petty, beyond the mundane of our egos that, due to fear, crave attention, are starving for validation, feel unsafe.

Fear is the reason. But most are unconnected to their fear. Most have gone far down the path of defensiveness—making someone else wrong because they are scared to surrender their image that they are in control. And their thought that control gets them somewhere.

Control is a result of fear trying to change a situation so that a person feels safe.

Look at a baby, a toddler. They are completely dependent on their caregivers. When the caregivers fail to sufficiently meet the little one's needs mentally, emotionally, or physically, the little one can get afraid and go into protection mode. We all know tantrums, withdrawal, etc.

We are built to try to survive. Mentally, we create scenarios that seem to explain to us why a scene is scary to us. And children often blame themselves for feeling so bad. There must be something wrong with them, they surmise. They don't have a bigger perspective. They don't know that the grownups just haven't figured out the best way to handle things.

Meditation: 12-13-2020

This morning getting my warm lemon juice to drink, I feel Saint Germain (Ascended One, like Jesus). My sense of his communication is, "Let me guide you." I agree. He's cool.

I sit down to meditate. "Get the book done."

DNA—I see my strands unwinding, dancing. All the epigenetic parts being activated appropriately with Light. Everyone's individual DNA dance.

I want everyone to upgrade, to grow, to Be, Feel the Light, the Love that is Everything.

I want the book to be encoded with codons, Light messages that go to the right people at the right time. Speaking to our DNA. Unwinding old messages and encoding with the true individual will of each human soul. With grace—effortless, sliding like melted butter into the right configuration for you.

Channel all my wonderful friends in my experience. First the book which will be a preview of smaller books to come. This book is an introduction to those wonderful friends in the Universe, in Creation. And then a book from the Elohim, from the Ascended Ones, from the Angels, from Galactic Light people.

I feel the motivation to write. As I sit and type, my son and his girlfriend are here being silly, making dinner, being in joy. Christmas lights are on in the house, and I am reminded of myself as a seven-month-old with croup being so mesmerized by the Christmas lights on the tree that I stopped coughing.

The magic of light and color. The Color Kittens that my dad loved reading to me as a child. Light. Dancing colors. DNA dancing. Color-coded codons of DNA dancing, creating joy and gladness. The power of love is joy.

Today is Sunday, a day when many Light Beings, like Archangels Michael and Faith, strongly beam to Earth the blue Light energy from Source. Blue is a vibration that brings power (protection) and faith. Through power and a feeling of safety, we have faith, we trust. Through faith, love. All intersperses and encircles. All is love. Love is all there is.

2021 arrives! What a year 2020 was.

26

Interdimensional Walkabout

It's two months later and I sit down to reflect.

As I have grown in my own unique spiritual way, I find that Spirit appears in my awareness at random moments throughout the day.

So, more regularly from this point on in this composition, *songs* from meditations will be included that have led me back to contributing to this *symphony*. I am trusting that Spirit is in charge and that there is a bigger view of what needs to happen here.

Meditation Notes: Archangel Faith,
partner of Archangel Michael, emerges

Most who are so inclined know of the male Archangels: Michael, Raphael, Gabriel, Uriel, and on. Few have heard of the female Archangels.

I discovered that the females had chosen to not be front and center for this planet, mainly because this planet has been male-oriented.

I imagine that they have been waiting for the appropriate moment in our evolution to be more visible. They have always been active.

Now the receptive, feminine energy is taking on a more visible role in the world and I feel our beautiful female Archangels have chosen to join that visibility on the spiritual plane.

Archangel Faith this morning gifted me with her Light. She and Archangel Michael work through the blue ray, the energy of Divine Will or intent or action or movement forward or power or protection.

Many call on Archangel Michael for protection. And as you feel protected, you feel safe. Through feeling safe and experiencing that safety, you grow trust in the one who keeps you safe. In this case, in Archangel Michael. Another word for trust could be faith. You have faith that you are safely, personally taken care of.

Archangel Faith embodies the quality of trust and facilitates the development of the emotion of trust in us for the Divine. Being trustworthy is one characteristic of the Divine.

How did I, a product of atheists, come to trust in the Divine?

I was, and am, a work in progress. Over the years the Divine, in many forms, reached out to me, in ways that fit my nature—from wondering in tenth grade if my parents knew the truth about Spirit, to finding and reading many books that spoke of spiritual topics, to having an experience with the powerful energy of Jesus touching my forehead, to being hit with a wall of loving energy inviting me to meditate in Old Saint Mary's Church in San Francisco (explained more later), to many other experiences that invited, that welcomed, that loved, that energized, that gave me peace.

Today I welcome and live in, depend on, and love the connection with Spirit in all Her forms. She can be Angels, Galactic Light Beings (like the Arcturians, a fifth-dimensional group of beings who embody how Love works in a community), Elohim (Light Beings who create form from Light), or Ascended Masters (folks who have lived on the earth and are now helping us evolve into our Light Self), and many of the other manifestations of Creation, both on Earth and in other dimensions.

I revel in the diversity! It's so much fun to explore, to discover, to make the acquaintance of new and varied life forms of the Universe(s).

I grow and expand as I am in the presence of, among so many, the Arcturians (Galactic Light Beings), Djwahl Kuhl (Ascended One), Vywamus (Galactic Light Being), Melchizedek (CEO of the Universe), the multi-universal Logos (the Light community in charge of universes), the Council of Twelve before the Throne (Light Beings close to the heart of Source), and, of course, Source.

Each one has their individual personality, heart, and way of doing things.

I love discovering Saint Germain's penchant for acting! For being so enthusiastic and having a great sense of humor.

Or the incredible heart of Vywamus, the higher aspect of Sanat Kumara the head of the Arcturians. I am overcome with the love of this being.

Or the vast Intelligent Mother Hen-like energy of Melchizedek.

Or the sincere, respectful, focused enthusiasm of Dr. Lorphan (a doctor who has helped many of us in healing) from Sirius, whom we can call on to help in our healing.

What a vast family we are part of!

And how do I know all these folks? Because I trust I am safe in this exploration. My solo trip in Europe in 1968 was preparing me for many journeys into the unknown.

I begin my spiritual meditations by creating space, envisioning, intending, and speaking of the forms of protection that will ensure that what I feel, see, and hear is of Source. (Please do what works for you.)

There are many ways to create spiritual space. I have a few that I'm using these days. One is the blue flame armor shield of Archangels Michael and Faith.

As I work with clients inviting in Divine Light to support them, their feedback is most often, "I feel so much calmer."

As I have been supported, I love to support and introduce others to the joy and majesty, the gentleness and power, and the love of the unseen Divine.

My dad would say, "If you can't prove it by science, then it doesn't exist." I think quantum mechanics and quantum physics are getting closer to making scientific connections that speak to aspects of this sustained creation energy.

Einstein, even though he had problems with quantum theory, wrote: "The most beautiful thing we can experience is the mysterious. It is the source of all true art and science." (Rowe and Schulmann 2007, 229)

If you feel like it, invite Archangel Faith into your life. Just see what happens. You could envision her immersed in blue light or fire.

My goal for this manual is to bring to you, dear reader, a sense of the Other—a felt or seen or heard or known sense. Since we all experience differently, my hope is that as you read these words, they will become a transmission of more than visual stimuli acting upon your cerebral cortex.

My hope is that these words help you to connect even more intimately with Love in all its forms and that you experience more calm, more love, more freedom, more gratitude, more healing, and more abundance in the ways that best serve you.

Meditation: 3-14-2021

Dancing with the fifth-dimensional chakras with the help of Djwahl Kuhl, The Arcturians, Vywamus, the Angels, and Metatron, head of Archangels.

We have seven basic three-dimensional chakras, the ones most people are familiar with.

When we connect with more expanded versions of ourselves, we encounter chakras associated with other dimensions—fourth and fifth dimensions, for instance. I got my information from Joshua David Stone's writings. (You can find many books by him on spirituality.) Other people may have different takes on this subject. It's all good. Take what works for you.

Melchizedek brings in his Golden dome of Light. The Elohim (Light beings who create form from Light) Hercules and Amazonia support the Blue Ray of Divine Power, as do Archangels Michael and Faith and the Ascended Master, El Morya.

I am invited to begin with light violet-white and then not go in order of the chakras, starting at the base of the spine, but starting at the crown (top of the head)—Platinum. And then I feel magenta—in the combination of the heart and the solar plexus.

The chakras dance together, interweaving with each other. The Angels and Masters are stitching together my fifth dimension chakras with my four main bodies—physical, emotional, mental, and astral. I can be fully Platinum vibration or magenta light.

Meditation: 3-21-2021

I am visited by Lenduce (the higher aspect of Vywamus, who is the higher aspect of Sanat Kumara, the leader of the Arcturians, the Galactic fifth dimensional community, at this juncture). I have never encountered this expanded being before. He (because that's as I experience him as a he) told me it's time to expand more.

I have been working with the fifth dimensional chakras for a couple months and they feel amazing! That is the level of Christ (or pure Love) Consciousness.

I have felt by installing, activating, and maybe, if I'm ready, beginning to utilize some of the mission work of one or more of these energy centers, that I am definitely expanding in consciousness.

I am aware of more of the state of being "in the world but not of it," as Jesus propounded. For instance, I have less interest in almost all the Netflix shows. I'm gravitating to the comedians on YouTube or documentaries.

And when folks on my Facebook feed make statements that I don't agree with, instead of reacting, I just notice where they're at, and move on.

I find I'm more able to have a broader view of my clients (today I am a spiritual psychotherapist) and am more easily able to see what they're about. I feel deeply about what I see as inequities in the world, but I'm not spending a lot of time lamenting about it. I look to Spirit to advise me on the best way I can contribute to the love in the world.

Lenduce showed me elements of the ninth dimension of creation, that point before the tenth dimension where form dissolves into the formless.

I saw possibilities of creation that are available to all of us. For instance, there were trees of undulating, multicolored trunks and branches that looked like rays of light. These kept shifting according to what the tree wanted to do in the moment.

I saw animals, also as multi-colored rays of light that shifted with ease into other animals. Some I did not recognize.

I saw plants that shifted into animals and into beings, not unlike humans.

And then he showed me temples of healing that were more advanced, closer to the energy of Source. Others we may have intuited and visited in meditation, like with the Pleiadians or the

Arcturians. He made sure I knew none was better than another, just different.

These temples seemed very close to the effervescent, continually regenerating core of Source. I could hear the hum, the primordial sound, that seems to hold the universe together, to sustain creation.

I could sense the direct transmission of Light straight from the heart of Source. The Light was a vast column of gently undulating, multi-varied, colored rays of light. He said these temples are available to all of us through our intent and asking of our guides.

Placing myself in the center of one of these temples (I am reminded of Sant Keshavadas who coined the phrase "Temple of Cosmic Religion") was like being in a whirlwind of energy so powerful that I wouldn't have been able to exist in it in one conscious piece if Lenduce had not shielded me with his own cloak of energy.

Because of this gifted shield, I was able to hear voices, so many voices, so many languages of Light that were talking simultaneously, like wheels of creation, providing the intelligence, the direction, the power, the love language to sustain creation. I heard voices from every corner of the universe, from all civilizations, providing the fantastic diversity that is needed to complete the Divine Plan.

"In all things, be grateful," has been a phrase that comes to me periodically. Where my heart softens into gratitude, my body relaxes, and I am humbled by the immense number of gifts I have. No less than the gift of my very existence.

Every so often, I am amazed that I Am, that I can reflect, that I can grow, that I can laugh, love, dance, hear, see, feel, and on and on and on. The sheer multiplicity of possibilities that I am living in astounds me.

That I have a cup from which to drink water. That I have windows on my house. That my feet can walk on grass. And on.

The temples that Lenduce showed me were also to demonstrate the possibilities for all of us; potentialities that we can create.

We each can connect with the Grand Creator and bring Heaven here to Earth. That is Creator's intent, per Lenduce, to me. These temples are available to all, for the health of all. We are each invited to grow to our fullest extent.

Back to Bisbee!

Is your head spinning with my back and forth!? This is sometimes how I roll. It is not meant to confuse you. See if you can go with the flow.

27

More Arizona Fun and Spirit Intervenes When We're Off Track

Other adventures while in Bisbee meant hiking and camping. A wonderful place is the Chiricahua Mountains on the border between Arizona and New Mexico. North to south, it spans forty miles; east to west, it covers twenty miles and encompasses four climatic zones. The name came from the Apache language and means "mountain." Geronimo fought the U.S. Government forces there.

We traveled to Portal, a tiny, unincorporated community in Cochise County on the border of New Mexico. From there, we would go to the American Museum of Natural History's Research Station. We camped in that vicinity and woke up to hummingbirds suspended over our faces, curiously observing us strange new specimens.

One extremely ill-advised excursion involved me and a friend. (It was his idea. Really!) We decided to hike up one of the mountains, camp for thirty days, and do a fast. We were into spiritual cleansing. Uh-huh.

We prepared everything: tent, sleeping bags, clothes, water purifiers, etc. We packed our backpacks, drove to Portal, and began our hike. It was a pretty tough hike with full backpacks, all uphill. I don't remember which hike we took. It could have been McCord Peak or Silver Peak.

What I do remember is that it was hard. Maybe three or four hours later, we got to the top. We set up our tent and got inside. I heard sounds of soft something landing on the outside of our tent. It had started to snow. In the summer.

We thought, *Oh, it won't go on for too long. This is summer!*

When the flakes became blobs thick and fast, we knew that that was that. Our thirty-day fast was over in one hour. We were not prepared for winter!

We put essentials in our backpacks, left the tent, and ran down the mountain. Needless to say, it took half the time. We found a lovely woman who lived in Portal and had an empty trailer. She let us hang out there for a few days while we recovered, mostly our pride.

When my friend had sufficiently recovered his energy, he went back up the mountain to take down the tent. Then we went back to Bisbee and food! There are other ways to cleanse spiritually.

Looking back, I think the benevolent Spirit of the Chiricahuas sent the snow. They couldn't let two young folks mess up their lives with such foolishness. Thank Goodness!

Janice had settled into Bisbee life and had decided to stay. I was feeling a bit itchy to move on back to California. I felt I needed to get on with life somehow and that Bisbee was not my last stop.

But first I wanted to spend some time in Sedona.

My friend Bill and I had bought a Ford pickup. We put a shell on the back, with a raised bed so you could sleep off the floor of the truck. Lying down on the bed put you in pretty close contact with the roof of the truck. If I were sleeping next to the cab, a bit of claustrophobia crept in, so I made sure I always slept at the back edge of the bed.

Bill was going back to California. I was going to spend a few months in Sedona.

It was coming into winter.

Intending to live in the truck, I drove the green pickup up Interstate 10, (about five hours) and landed in Sedona.

This was 1977. There were not too many parking rules. I found a beautiful place to park right up against the majestic red rocks in Red Rock Canyon and that's where I stayed most of my winter in Sedona.

It was a time among the New Age folks where there was a lot of talk about the coming earth changes: seas would rise, coasts and islands would disappear. It would herald a change on the earth where peace and love would prevail.

I attended some of these channelings where people would give dates when Japan would sink into the ocean, when the California coast would also submerge, etc. All to take place in the 1970s and '80s.

I remember being skeptical, because I had had my own experiences in Bisbee of tuning into an energy that communicated information not known before about folks I knew, for instance.

The tenor of these climate change channelings seemed to always sound the same. There was a ring of canned repetitiveness that I noticed. I went to hang out because I wanted to be around other folks who were interested in spirituality, but I wasn't convinced that it was real. It seemed to be programmed or involving an ego state in the messenger. And, it turned out, none of the timed predictions came true.

Now, of course, we have global warming telling us much the same thing about ocean levels rising, but in a factual, evidenced report. These channeled reporters were probably tuning into an energy that predicted climate change, but the timing and actual information were way off.

During my winter in Sedona, it snowed. Gorgeous! Snow on the red rocks!

I was cozy warm in my truck, crocheting a sweater for my sister. I decided to follow my own pattern and just put in whatever color whenever I felt like it. It took most of the winter. The sweater was long, and to my eyes, beautiful. So many bright colors. I was excited to give it to her.

28

Spirit Guides You and It's Not Always to Your Liking

After a few months in Sedona, it was time to move back to California. I was invited by my friend Bill to share a house in South San Francisco, on Byxbee Street (who would have guessed?) near San Francisco State University.

I needed a job. I had worked temp jobs as a typist in the past. I tried to teach myself shorthand and got a few characters down but wasn't proficient in the least. I decided to apply for secretary jobs because those paid more than just typing. I had never been a secretary, but I determined I could figure out the job. How hard could it be?

Because of fate or Spirit or just dumb luck, I landed a job at Hitachi America downtown on the seventh floor of the Pyramid building. I was the only white person working there that I noticed.

My boss was a kind man named Jiro. His office was in a small, glassed-in cubicle maybe six or eight feet from my desk. Other offices were adjacent to his.

There were only two problems with this position. One was that I didn't seem able to get to work exactly on time at 8:30 a.m. I was regularly two, five, or ten minutes late. The bosses were very kind about it but kept emphasizing that I needed to be early or exactly on time. I never really mastered the early/on-time criteria until I had my own business. Hmm. What was that about?

The other dilemma was that my boss smoked, and the secondhand smoke wafted right out his door and into my desk area. After my quick cigarette trial in Europe, I have never liked the smell of smoke, even less breathing it in.

I finally had to tell them that I would have to leave this job because of the smoke.

Well, the most amazing thing happened. Jiro's boss decided that Jiro needed to quit smoking. The whole group got together to support him, like a family doing an intervention with love.

Jiro was actively encouraged and rewarded with kudos, presents, and parties as he embarked on saying sayonara to his attachment. It was positive, cheerful, and super affirming for me too. Jiro was successful and I was smoke-free.

Spirit Finds a Way

During lunch hour on California Street, I would walk up the hill to get some exercise.

One lunchtime, I walked up seven blocks and found a sweet little church that turned out to be Old St. Mary's, a Catholic church.

(Sarah and I had explored different churches in Cambridge. We would walk into the place of worship and stay a while. We had decided that the only ones where we felt energy or a presence of something other than regular life were the Catholic ones.)

I walked up the steps of the church and opened the big front door. I was instantly hit with a wall of loving, welcoming energy. It kind of blew me away; it felt powerful, like a force field. (Kind of like the energy with Jesus that stopped my lunch in my backyard in Cambridge.)

I went inside and sat in a pew. No one else was in there. The walls were painted with beautiful frescoes of religious scenes and people. I was unfamiliar with the scenes, though I could recognize Jesus.

As I sat there, I continued to feel the warm, welcoming energy that filled my body and mind and brought peace. I felt like it was an invitation to keep coming in to sit.

So, I did. Every lunch hour, I went to sit in Old St. Mary's and every time I felt welcomed and supported by some unseen power—more invitation by Spirit to explore this world.

I left that Hitachi America job, not because of the people, but because I was getting bored. I guess I had mastered enough of that kind of secretarial work.

As I reflect on my ventures over the years, I notice that I have flourished with interesting challenges. When I feel there is nothing more to learn, I feel the need to move on.

Well, I decided to try my hand at being a higher-end secretary. I applied for and again, by some grace of Light, with no experience, was hired as a legal secretary in a probate law firm. I knew nothing about probate or law or any of it.

This was a firm run by two Italian brothers, with one other lawyer onboard. I was the secretary of the boss, Lorenzo. This job was a bit more challenging. I had to take dictation to type up letters. Well, that was fun as I wrote as fast as I could, creating my own shorthand. I tried to teach myself more traditional shorthand, but I wasn't getting it.

I must have done ok, or my boss was very forgiving because I worked in that job until I was ready to leave.

I learned things about probate, one of which was that probate attorneys can make a lot of money because the law guarantees them a percentage of the estate they administer. These attorneys had a good amount of wealthy Italian clients.

I also learned that Lorenzo loved sitting in the nearby coffee house for extended periods, shooting the breeze and talking about his escapades in WWII with his cronies. I periodically had to go get him—because of a client phone call, or something else he had to take care of—and take him away from his doughnuts.

During my sojourn into part of the legal world, I was also exploring more about crystals, healing modalities, and other spiritual disciplines.

I got acupuncture at the Haight Ashbury Clinic. I look at acupuncture as a spiritual discipline because it addresses mind, body, emotion, color, seasons, tastes, and more, and sees the interconnectedness of all with the natural world. Harmonizing ourselves with nature balances us with Spirit.

I meditated at the Zen Center in downtown San Francisco. I read more spiritual books. I learned more about herbs, food for health, and ways to detox.

I became friends with Elijah, an acupuncturist. He knew a guy named Ron who wanted to learn acupressure. Elijah was aware I knew something about acupressure and introduced us with the idea that I could teach him.

Ron came over to my house and we had classes. Classes became more than that and we started liking each other. Liking each other became more than that and we started dating. It became rather intense.

Ron was Catholic and introduced me to the Catholic mass.

The first time I had been to a Catholic mass was when I was maybe twelve. My friend, Margie, was Catholic and for some reason, I went to mass with her one day.

This would have been about 1960 or so. In those years, priests still did the mass in Latin.

I stood in the back of the church and watched the show; these guys had long dresses on and spoke a language no one understood. People were standing up, sitting down, kneeling, and then up and down again. I thought it was weird.

But Ron was very devout. He was also open to alternative spiritual styles. I thought that was cool.

He thought I had my spiritual hand in too many pots and needed to pick one.

Different dramas happened with Bill, who got jealous (even though Bill and I weren't an item, but it turned out he was quite attached to me). I moved out (another drama) and stayed with Ron's friends in another part of the city.

Ron and I were getting closer. He was called to work with the youth at St Joseph's Church in Marysville, California. He asked if I wanted to move with him. I said yes.

His parents, sister, and brother-in-law lived there, so we would have a place to stay.

We moved in with his sister and brother-in-law.

The pastor at St. Joseph's at that time was Monsignor Schons, a tall German fellow with a commanding and kind presence.

Ron became very involved in working with the monsignor and the youth. After a time, the monsignor found out that we were living together. That wasn't going to cut it with the church rules; Ron wasn't being a good example to the kids.

Ron had to make a choice: either we would stay together, and he would quit the church job, or we wouldn't live together, and he would stay with the job.

Well, for him the church was the stronger pull. We had to live apart.

I moved into a duplex in Yuba City (next door to Marysville), right down the street from a Sikh Temple. The house had a six-foot wooden fence all around the very large backyard.

I was pissed that someone else should dictate our lives and felt that anger for a while. In retrospect, it was for the best and Spirit was guiding all along. But I didn't know that then.

While Ron was working with the monsignor and deciding where that would lead him, I began attending mass with his family on Sundays.

His dad was very connected to the Sacred Heart of Jesus and had painted a picture of how that felt to him. It hung over their fireplace—very beautiful.

Over time, I became more curious about this Catholic thing. I was experiencing my own pull into the essence of this energy. I started reading about the saints—Bernadette of Lourdes, Teresa of Lisieux, Clare of Assisi, and Teresa of Avila.

What struck me most was the personal relationship each of them had with Christ or God. It reminded me of the personal relationship with Spirit that Bhakti Yoga teaches. For these women, it was all about the heart, the love, the connection.

I also read the Desert Fathers. They were part of the Eastern Church.

Thomas Merton wrote of the Desert Fathers of the fourth century AD.

"They sought a way to God that was uncharted and freely chosen, not inherited from others who had mapped it out beforehand. They sought a God whom they alone could find, not one who was given, in a set stereotyped form by somebody else." (Merton 1960)

"Mysticism," according to author Dana Greene, "is not some rare, esoteric phenomenon, but rather a movement of the heart, open to all, fully realized by the few, in which the object, method, and consequence are all the same. To seek, to find, to be transformed by that which is eternal and fully real, the One, which the mystics call God." (Greene 1987)

A few concepts from their writing follow and express what drew me to read about them.

The Desert Fathers practiced Hesychasm, a Greek word for "stillness, rest, quiet, and silence."

This practice was primarily about creating interior silence and continual prayer with eyes closed—empty of mental pictures and visual concepts, but with the intense consciousness of God's presence.

The Eastern mystics believed that the supreme spiritual experience would be a vision of the Divine and Uncreated Light.

This was identical to the Jewish Shekinah and the light witnessed by the three disciples that surrounded Jesus on Mt. Tabor at His transfiguration.

Because God is Light (1 John 1:5), the experience of those energies was said to take the form of light.

Even though this Light is not a sensible or material light, it can be seen by the inner eye when a person has developed this skill.

Prayer was the total response of human beings to God, and one did not pray merely with the mind or the lips. Through discipline, prayer became a spontaneous offering of the whole being of humanity.

Here is an excerpt from St. John Chrysostom that expresses some of the heart of these mystics.

St. John Chrysostom, whose liturgy is celebrated in Eastern Orthodox Churches and Roman Catholic Churches of the Byzantine Rite, and whose eloquence and pragmatism made him the most outstanding leader of the Eastern Church, wrote in his Seventh Discourse on 2 Corinthians:

Do you wish to see how their inner light penetrates even through their bodies? "And looking steadfastly on Stephen, they saw his face as it had been the face of an angel" (Acts 6:15) ... But this is as nothing compared with the glory which shone within him. For what Moses showed in his face, they carried in their souls...And much more than that, for what Moses had was more physical, whereas this was spiritual...Just as bodies which can receive and reflect light, when illumined by self-radiant bodies, themselves pour their reflected light on other bodies close to them, so it is with believers...God appears to the mind in the heart, at first as a flame purifying its lover, and then as a light which illumines the mind and renders it God-like. (Schaff 1887, 314)

Like some of the above mystics, I wasn't interested in Church doctrine, but I was very interested in creating that same relationship with Spirit that I had found in their writings.

As I read about the mystics' hearts longing for the Spirit, I felt my own heart respond. The longing became intense to feel, to sense, to know God.

So, though I didn't agree with some of the ways of the Church, I was curious to see how it would feel to receive the Eucharist, to dive deeper into those rituals.

I decided I would get baptized.

Monsignor Schons was extremely generous. Instead of directing me to the usual classes that one takes to enter the church, he had me read a book about Edith Stein.

Edith Stein was a Polish Jew who became an atheist as a teenager. She later studied and converted to Catholicism. She and her sister were taken to Auschwitz where she created meditation and prayer groups for the women there.

At that time, I read no further than her biography. I didn't delve into her written works. As I read more about her now forty years later, I am curious and will explore her work further on empathy, embodiment, emotions, personhood, collective intentionality, and the nature of the state.

Perhaps the monsignor sensed some similarity between Edith Stein and me.

I am part Jew, grew up in an atheist household, and now, many years later work in a job that deals in empathy, the emotions, and personhood. I am pursuing embodiment and collective intentionality and learning about the nature of the state.

As I hope you, dear reader, are growing from these words and how they affect you, so I, too, am growing as I write. I am humbled and love how Spirit sees the big picture of where we need to go and gives us signposts along the way. We choose to follow them or not.

I grew up playing the piano. At some point as a teenager, I taught myself the notes of the guitar and learned a few chords. I never was able to master bar chords!

At St. Joseph's Church in Marysville, there was no music for the mass. Somehow or other, a couple of friends and I decided we would be the music. I was the guitar player (very basic!) and the three of us were the choir. I taught them the songs and we even learned harmonies. At times others joined us, but we three were the core.

There was also a Spanish mass on Sunday. They needed a guitar player (again, five or six chords seemed to work for most songs) and asked me. I thought, *How fun!* and agreed. They taught me the Spanish songs for the mass. I understood some of the meaning or got the gist, but I was able to sing the songs because my brain could make it work when the words were combined with music!

Many Sundays, I played for two masses.

In Catholicism, besides baptism, there is also a confirmation ceremony. The church sees confirmation as a sacrament created by Jesus. It gifts wisdom, understanding, knowledge, counsel, fortitude, piety, and devotion to God to the previously baptized person. It is performed by a bishop through laying on of hands and anointing the forehead with oil.

At that time, the bishop of the Sacramento diocese was Bishop Frances Quinn. He was a loving, kind, spiritual man.

St. Joseph's was planning a confirmation event. Monsignor Schons decided that it was time for me to be confirmed. So, as usual in the mass, I (and my singing colleagues) played and sang. At my own confirmation!

30

Work as Spiritual Practice

Time and events marched on. Ron decided he wanted to become a priest. I had settled into my little duplex in Yuba City.

I also needed a job. I trained for and then drove for Dial-A-Ride, the small bus that picks up people at their homes to drive them places.

It was fun using walkie-talkies, with "10-4" and that kind of talk. I remember one day it was raining like crazy. I pulled over on a shoulder to make a U-turn to leave someone off in front of their house. My two right wheels got completely stuck in the mud. I couldn't move. I called in to the office and they sent out another bus, but that bus couldn't get me unstuck. The passengers got on the other bus.

Finally, a guy in a big pickup truck with a winch and a heavy metal cable attached saw me and stopped to help. He hooked up to the front end of the bus and, *voila*, pulled me right out of the deep mud! The kindness of strangers!

Well, driving a little bus wasn't fulfilling some other needs and I also needed more income for expenses.

Yuba College, a community college in Marysville, had an LVN program. I thought a good next step would be to become a nurse.

I signed up and began the year-and-a-half program. It was fairly easy because I had taken biology in college.

Some of the nursing practice work at the local hospital was comical.

The first time I was supposed to give someone a shot, I filled the syringe, cleaned the skin in their gluteal (butt) area, and thrust the needle.

It bounced off.

I was mortified. Now what?!

The instructor said, "Just push it in." And I did. It went in!

The patient didn't jump or anything. After that, it was easier.

There were many other first times: Like putting in catheters in men or women—each one very different, of course. Or doing dressing changes. Or cleaning up messes of all kinds. Or helping people to the bathroom. There are so many tasks in nursing to take care of a person.

Nurses are such a gift. They need to be completely appreciated and compensated appropriately.

After graduating from LVN school, I got a job as a nurse's aide at Fremont, the hospital in Yuba City.

I took my LVN boards, passed, and was upgraded to working as an LVN. We did everything that RNs do but under the supervision of the RN. We couldn't start IV lines unless we had taken an extra course.

I worked all the floors: pediatrics, general nursing, ICU, recovery room, and ER. When I was working in ICU, the RNs there said, "Why don't you get your RN?" I could do it like they did. I researched their idea and thought, *Why not?*

There was an off-campus nursing program from the Regents Program of the State University of New York, in Albany. They have the same programs today.

If you were from out of state, you could participate in the programs by taking tests locally and it would be as if you had attended classes for the RN.

I applied and got in; my biology and chemistry in college helped. I took six multiple-choice tests on different nursing subjects. I passed. It was as if I had taken six different RN courses

Then one weekend, I went to Stanford University Hospital for the practical exam.

We worked with patients in their hospital. I did a sterile dressing change, made an IV calculation and hung meds, gave oral meds, did a bed bath, and took care of two patients.

I passed. So, from the six tests and the one practical exam, it was as if I had successfully completed RN nursing school. It all went reasonably smoothly because I had so much real-time hospital experience. My ICU nurses knew what they were about!

Then I went on to the state boards. Those were harder, but I passed.

As an RN I could do more, like be a charge nurse for a general nursing section. I was the charge nurse sometimes, but it wasn't my favorite thing to do. You had to call doctors and run the place. I was more into patient care.

We were working at the beginning of the AIDS epidemic. Not much was known about the disease at the time, but it was postulated that it was spread by bodily fluids or blood. One night, while working the 3 p.m. to 11 p.m. shift, I had an AIDS patient.

None of the other nurses would even go into his room. The staff had been avoiding him all day. I was aghast. He was a human being! I was pretty sure if you gave him a back rub or handed him his dinner tray, you were not going to catch AIDS.

So, I did give him a back rub and took care of him like all my other patients.

On another day, I had a patient who had had abdominal surgery and had a very large dressing (bandage) on their stomach. On my shift, the dressing was soaked in blood. I knew that was bad; something had broken loose. I called the surgeon (one of the two best in the hospital at the time).

I'm not known for my detailed descriptions on a good day. I told him that there was "a whole big bunch of blood on the dressing."

There was silence on the other end. And then he said, "A whole big bunch?" He was trying not to be mean. So, I tried as best I could to guess the inches that it covered. I think it was ten.

Of course, as a charge nurse, I had to learn to be specific. I hope I've gotten better at this over the years.

Being a nurse helped me feel that I was doing something good. We generally had five patients per shift, and I could manage that. Like all nurses, I saw all kinds of illnesses and dilemmas. I felt for everyone in pain.

One night, I had a patient who was dying of cirrhosis. He had been a drinker. He needed me to listen. He told me about all the times he wished he had done things differently with his family, and about his regrets. I sat with him. My heart deeply felt his sadness.

That night at home, before bed, I prayed for him with all my heart. I sent soul-felt prayers to Spirit that he would get what he needed. I found out later that he died during my prayer time.

Spiritual Safaris

This was also a time when I kept exploring my spirituality. I wanted to find out how these mystics connected to the Divine. I sought out and went on several retreats—sometimes led, sometimes solo.

I visited the Benedictines at Big Sur. Their place is cool. You could have your own little cabin. They would leave your meals on your front steps, or you could join them in silent meals. You could have as much solitude as you wanted. And you could join the monks at their multiple prayer times.

I loved the solitude at their monastery, going for walks around the grounds and out toward the cliffs overlooking the ocean.

I also visited Our Lady of the Redwoods in Northern California. Here was a small group of sisters of the Cistercian Order who lived simply. The Trappists in Vina, California, called them their radical sisters. I loved their simplicity.

They provided a small hut for each visitor. You could attend their early morning Buddhist sit in the chapel or go to mass. You joined them for the silent meals, where everyone bussed their own dishes and contributed to cleaning up.

The surroundings were beautiful. I walked their grounds near the Redwoods, taking in the silence.

Ron had introduced me to the Trappists at New Clairvaux Monastery in Vina, California. He loved one of the monks, Father Timothy, who was a great mentor for his spiritual growth.

I went up to Vina on my own when they allowed women to stay overnight. I joined them for prayer in the chapel and walked around their orchard. This quote from their website spoke truth to me then as it does today.

> Guided by the light of the Divine inside of you, you may be drawn to read a specific book in the library, or write your thoughts and feelings in a journal, or talk with a monk or friend you happened to meet. Perhaps you will be drawn to walk through the orchards or take a well-needed nap. You may simply feel the call to sit in attentive silence. Whatever opening may occur for you, know it is not an accident. Regardless of why you came here, your silence and your deep listening will allow you to hear God's voice in a new way. As the Psalms challenge us: Be still and know that I am God (Ps. 46:10). (www.newclairvaux.org/visit)

I attended a guided silent retreat at St. Clare's Retreat in the Santa Cruz mountains with a friend. We got so giddy with the spiritual energy that we found ourselves laughing uproariously for long periods. It was hard to maintain silence, we felt so much joy.

I went to San Damiano, the Franciscan center in Danville, California.

I visited the Sisters of Mercy in Newcastle, California, for several guided retreats. Some of their sisters live in houses in Sacramento.

From books and retreats and a hunger in my soul and heart for spiritual connection, I wondered if I could be a nun.

I talked with Father Bishop of St. Ignatius Church in Yuba City, CA. He directed me to talk with the Sisters of Mercy.

The Mercys originated in Ireland and have founded convents in many areas of the world. Their order developed by teaching orphaned young girls and feeding the poor. Later, they moved into the area of healthcare.

I talked with a sister about my feelings. We met several times and then I decided to give the Mercys a try.

To enter the order, you must take the MMPI (Minnesota Multiphasic Personality Inventory). It's a long multiple-choice test that pretty accurately determines if you're crazy or off your rocker somehow, or if you are a good match for being a nun.

The sister that I was communicating with directed me to a psychologist who would administer it. But...it cost $500. I didn't have that kind of money at the time.

I had been attending mass at St. Isadore's Catholic Church in Yuba City. Father Bishop was the priest in charge at that time. One of my friends, Mateo, encouraged me to ask Father Bishop if he would loan me the money. Hesitantly, I did. And that generous priest GAVE me the $500. Wow.

I took the MMPI over a two-day period. When I returned to the doctor's office to learn of the results, the psychologist concluded that I would try out convent life, but I wouldn't stay, that I wasn't exactly built for that life. I was more of a free spirit, and I liked variety and adventure.

Well, okay. I was ready to try this next adventure.

The Mercys were offering newbies a three-month trial period to see what they felt about this life.

At that time, the Mercys' San Juan Hospital in Sacramento had a convent attached. I signed up for the summer.

The convent housed about twenty sisters then. We each had a room, dormitory style. There was one long corridor, each side with ten or so rooms. I had a room in the middle.

My room was next to Sister Ava (a nun from a different order who wanted to work in healthcare, and so had joined the Mercys for a while). Down the hall from me was Sister Amelia. These two ladies kept me sane for the summer.

I had learned the yang style of Tai Chi from my friend Ron, and when Ava and Amelia found out, they wanted to learn it. So, I became a Tai Chi teacher!

This was my social interaction for three months.

I soon found out there wasn't to be much interaction between me and the sisters, or even, it appeared, among the sisters themselves. That had not been my expectation or desire. I wanted to learn from them, to hear how they felt, what was easy and hard for them, what was in their hearts and minds and bodies. It wasn't to be.

I talked with the sister in charge about this. She said this was the way it was, and I would get used to it. I thought *I don't think so.*

I felt very isolated that summer.

While living in Yuba City, I had adopted a stray dog. My friend, Sophia, said he had been hanging around their house and I needed to claim him. I thought, *Yeah, right!*

But I drove over to her house to get a look at him. He was tall and skinny with brown, white, and black coloring. He looked like a cross between a wolf and a German Shepherd.

He had obviously not eaten for a long time. He was scared of people. Her kids started feeding him jellybeans and he sat down in the street to eat them. It didn't take long before I knew I did need to adopt him.

He let us get close to him when he was eating the jellybeans, so we were soon able to lift him up and put him in the back of a pickup truck. I drove him to my house with its large backyard and six-foot fence all around. I had to carry him to put him in the yard.

I named him Jeremiah after Jeremiah in the Bible who was a prophet in the Old Testament. For some reason, I was drawn to that name.

Well, my Jeremiah was a handful. He didn't let me touch or pet him for six months; he had apparently been so abused by humans. He would often somehow jump the six-foot fence and run away.

I would have to get in the car and go look for him. I always found him and somehow enticed him to get in the car, a Honda station wagon, and brought him home.

He was a big dog. When I walked him on a leash, folks would move to the other side of the street. He looked intimidating. He was a wimp.

He started fattening up a bit and needed exercise. Down the road a piece, there was a wild area with levees and grasses, a good place to run. I would put Jeremiah in the back of my Honda and drive to the levees, and we would run and walk until it was time for me to go to work at the hospital.

Jeremiah was in his element. He ran and ran. There were pheasants and he caught them. I would catch up with him and, much to his chagrin would make him drop them. They looked dead as they fell out of his mouth. But when I made him move away from them, they flew away.

Jeremiah was a free spirit. Running was a delight, but at some point, I had to go to work.

I'd call him, "Jeremiah! Come on, time to go." He wasn't having it. I tried a few more times. No go.

So, I decided to try something else. I got in my car and started driving away. He chased me. I stopped the car and said, "You ready?" Nope.

I would get back into my car and drive some more with him chasing after me. It often took two or three tries before he would jump into the back of the station wagon.

By some miracle, I wasn't ever late to work. Guess I learned something from Hitachi America.

While living at the Mercy convent, I got a call from the couple who were house-sitting my duplex in Yuba City. Jeremiah was always running away. They couldn't control him.

What to do? I asked the sisters if I could bring him to the convent. They had an outside courtyard that was surrounded by a very high concrete wall. I thought I could keep him there. To my surprise, they said yes! Generous hearts.

So, Jeremiah became a monk-dog at the Sisters of Mercy.

There were only a few issues.

Jeremiah decided that he owned the courtyard. Whenever the sisters were going from the convent through the courtyard to take a walk outside, Jeremiah would bark fiercely at them, but from a distance.

Some of the older nuns were intimidated and scurried out as fast as possible without looking at him. Such tolerance!

Sister Camila loved Jeremiah and helped me take him for walks. He had become human-tamed by then and loved being petted. I think Jeremiah brightened her day.

Once my large hunting dog found a skunk and the skunk let loose. Oh, no! What was I to do then? The courtyard was stinking up very powerfully.

I looked up cures. Tomato juice didn't work. Baths were no good. Finally, I called a vet who told me to soak him in vanilla. I bought a big bottle and poured it all over him, rubbing it in thoroughly.

Wow. That did the trick! Now he smelled like a vanilla cookie. Much better than skunk courtyard.

The sisters were extremely kind and patient with me and Jeremiah. I am grateful to them for that.

But then three months came to an end. I wasn't feeling so great about my nun experience. In talking to my sister-mentor, she said they wanted me to enter their order.

I decided I really couldn't. I wasn't feeling the spirit. So, I thanked them very much for letting me try out convent life and wished them well.

While I was experimenting with this spiritual lifestyle, my friend, Catherine, was doing the same. She was doing the three-month gig in a different Mercy convent. She liked it and she entered the order.

Catherine and I had so much fun. We laughed a lot and saw life similarly. We got each other.

But some of Catherine's partying had involved alcohol. It was hard for her to give it up, even in the convent. Several times, she came home late at night, drunk, at times leaving a mess behind her as she went up to her room. The sisters were not pleased. I believe it was then they asked her to leave.

Once I was giving her a massage and noticed a large lump in her breast. I said, "Catherine, did you know you have a lump?!"

She hadn't. The lump was cancer.

Catherine went through surgery and chemo, and then the cancer spread. Eventually, it went to her brain. She ended up in a nursing home in her forties. My Catherine was dying and not a nun anymore.

I had a friend with whom I meditated regularly. One evening, he came to my little house for meditation. I told him about Catherine. He suggested we meditate to help her transition. I agreed. The two of us moved into a deep meditation where we talked to her, saying it was okay to let go and let God, that her life was good, and she could move on. Later we found out that she died during that time.

I missed Catherine terribly. St. Francis Church in Sacramento held a mass for her. At that time, I was in the choir there, as was my friend, Elizabeth, the lady with the incredible voice.

I tried to sing for part of the mass but broke down sobbing. Elizabeth held me. So much gratitude for her.

32

Once Again, Source Intervenes

I had been in nursing for three years and then felt I wasn't growing or learning much. I was becoming bored.

One week in the summer of 1987, three separate people said to me that they thought I would be a good counselor (kind of out of the blue, so to speak). They weren't in cahoots.

That same week, I saw an ad in a Catholic newspaper about an orientation that Saturday for a University of San Francisco off-campus counseling program being held at St. Ignatius Church in Sacramento. I went. I thought, *this sounds good*.

I applied, sending in all my BA and AA records, and got in.

I started my MA that fall.

I commuted to St. Ignatius church from Yuba City, where our counseling classes were being held in Sacramento on Thursdays and some Saturdays. We had two classes for each of the trimesters. We had tests and papers, and no thesis.

Our teachers were local therapists who had become USF teachers.

Of course, I had to change my work. I became an IV therapist at Fremont Hospital. Talk about learning on the job! I worked three days a week in ten-hour shifts and got wonderful shoes because I was on my feet for the full ten hours.

I started IVs and hung IV meds. Sometimes I couldn't start the IV because the person's veins would roll or burst.

You were supposed to start at the hand. If you couldn't get into the vein there, you were to try a little higher.

Once I was trying to start an IV on an older woman who wasn't having it. She kept yelling, "You're killing me!" I think I've blocked out whether I got her needle in.

One thing I refused to do was put IVs in the kids or babies. I had no experience, and I didn't think I could handle it. Thank goodness the supervisor went along with me.

Being an IV therapist for three days a week was perfect. I was my own boss, I managed my own time, and it provided enough income to pay the bills and begin to pay for school. USF is expensive. Most of the student fees and tuition went on my credit card.

On my first day of school, I met Carly, a fellow student who was to become a dear friend.

Two years later in June of 1989, we got our diplomas, both of us earning MAs in counseling.

Meanwhile, in 1988, I moved to Sacramento. It was getting to be old commuting to grad school, and I felt that Yuba City had given me all she could. Sacramento seemed to offer more opportunities.

Carly worked with the Mental Health Association, and she found me a room with a former client of hers. Well, this roommate and I turned out to not be a match.

She was accepting, however, of having Jeremiah in the house; she had a dog too.

My roommate was jealous of most everything I did. I had my sister stay overnight on a visit. That was bad.

I didn't do this or that right. I needed to move out.

My friend from grad school, Sandra, was moving out of a little house and wondered if that would work for me. The moment I walked into that house that sat on a large backyard behind a main house, I knew. I felt a welcoming energy like I was home. To top it off, the towels were the same design my grandma had used. I felt her energy.

I decided to take it.

But there was one problem. They wouldn't allow pets. What was I to do with Jeremiah?

I put out ads for him and finally, a woman said she needed a watchdog. I told her that Jeremiah was basically a chicken, but he looked fierce. She thought that was just fine.

The day came and I drove him to her house in Auburn. He knew something was up. My heart was breaking. I found the place and put him on a leash. He attached himself to my leg.

I gave him to the lady, whom I liked.

I cried the whole way back to Sacramento. I'm surprised I could see where I was driving.

After moving into the little house, I needed a church to attend in Sacramento and St. Francis appealed to me. The Franciscans were nature people, liberal-minded, and accepted everyone, gay and straight, into their community. Father Benjamin was a priest there and had a reputation for being very ecumenical. He also had a counseling degree. I joined St. Francis and auditioned to sing in the choir.

This was big stuff compared to our tiny musical group in Marysville. We were a good-sized group with a pianist and a great director. I sang there for several years.

I also needed more active exploration into deeper spirituality.

I met a woman, Katherine, who was holding contemplative prayer groups at her house. The format was based on Father Thomas Keating's work with contemplative prayer. Katherine and I and sometimes another person met at her house on Saturday mornings to meditate in silence. It was glorious and deep.

I always wondered how Jeremiah was getting along.

One Saturday morning after prayer with Katherine, I went outside to get into my car. I got in and shut the driver's door. I looked right, onto Katherine's front lawn. There stood a dog that looked an awful lot like my Jeremiah.

As I watched, he looked at me and came around to the driver's door. My window was open. He put his paws on my windowsill. I petted and talked to him. I said how great he looked; pretty filled out and healthy with a collar and tags.

We chatted this way for a bit, and I decided that if this were Jeremiah, he was fine. I could relax and know that his life was good. How he had gotten from Auburn to there, I had no idea.

I pushed his paws off my sill, wished him blessings, and drove away. He chased after me.

I always thought that that was Source telling me that my beautiful, timid puppy was doing fine, and I could rest easy.

33

Giving Back to the Sisters

After my stint as a trial nun, one of the Sisters of Mercy asked me if I wanted to manage their infirmary at their motherhouse in Auburn, which is where the sisters were cared for when they were ill.

I said yes. I worked there for a year.

When I came on board, I was greeted by the lone LVN on staff. She filled me in on what had been going on. The rest of the staff were CNAs and others who were not trained in nursing but were caring for the nuns anyway.

One of her concerns was that the CNAs and non-schooled folk were giving out narcotics without knowing anything about them.

There had been other safety problems as well. The problems didn't stem from a lack of caring from the staff, just an absence of supervision and training.

I took the lay of the land and ascertained that we needed to hire licensed people, preferably LVNs, to administer all the meds and be in charge. That way, we had staff qualified to make informed medical decisions for the nuns' care, including, when necessary, calling doctors with appropriate information.

There was pushback from the head of the order. She said it was too expensive. I said it was a lawsuit waiting to happen. She wasn't willing. She called in their attorney to evaluate. He agreed with me. I began recruiting LVNs.

I reorganized the structure of the staffing. One LVN was on each shift—day, evening, and night. CNAs were the support staff. Folks who were not trained had to find other work.

There wasn't a lot of happiness with my decision from the staff, except from my original LVN.

Because at that time I was learning to be a therapist, I thought I could deal with the opposition from the staff. I created an open-door policy in my office.

People came in to voice their dismay. I listened and, hopefully, showed them empathy and understanding.

I told them that the restructure was for the safety of the nuns. After all, most of the staff felt affection for them and really did want them to be safe.

No one was outright obnoxious about it, but undoubtedly there were grumblings out of my earshot. I think people refrained from insurrection because they were in a convent and had respect for the nuns.

People settled into an uneasy readjustment, though it took time.

I made sure to celebrate everyone's birthdays, and plan gatherings to appreciate all their work.

During this revamping, I wrote out job and shift descriptions and created lists of doctors, as well as lists of other procedures that were commonplace in the care of the sisters.

I wanted to make this place run without me. After a year, it did.

I was getting tired of commuting forty minutes to Newcastle from Sacramento, and after a while, there really wasn't anything more for me to do. So, I decided it was time to move on.

There seems to be a theme here! I'm always after something more to learn, something else to challenge me.

How do you decide when you're ready for your next adventure? Does your inner voice keep talking to you about something more? Do you start feeling bored, or uncomfortable in your situation?

These feelings are worth paying attention to and considering. It could be a deeper part of you giving you good advice for your life.

Skip to Present Day

Birthday today. Seventy-three. Weird number. Taking care of myself—got a super relaxing facial. Tomorrow is a massage and this weekend we go to Mount Shasta.

In a meditation, I hear Saint Germain say, *"Even though the Human Design program says you are a projector (I wait for people to ask me to do something), your evolution involves continually reaching out to others in love, with your particular kind of love. Guidance, dedication, and persistence. You revel in helping people. You love when they succeed. If you can be of help, you are.*

Now we will lead you. Take my hand to the mountain top. (I assume he meant Mt. Shasta.) Let the mountain sustain you. Let her enter your consciousness and lift you higher.

In no way will you lose what you've gained. The door is open. Go through it. (And I do.)

This is the land of infinite possibilities where you will learn to dwell continuously. It's a land of peace. It's harmonious. It's from whence all things arise.

Watch your ideas take shape and move like feathers into other realms to blossom into art, music, life. ALL things are possible. In joy. And Stillness.

All things are manifest in bubbles of exuberant joy. The creation process is joy. The idea emerges. The bubble rises. It pops and creates gales of laughter. It spreads its essence and pollinates all it's meant to touch. Bits of joyful inspiration seeding a thought, a heart, a gut instinct.

In all things, be grateful and all will be added unto you.

There is a bit of truth in all religions. And yet all religions are not needed. The truth is you and creation. You are Creation. You are the All.

There is no arrogance in this. This is simple truth. Simple humility, simple joy.

You are all that is needed. You and your friends, all you touch, so much joy, so much light.

From one speck of light comes a universe of Light and all that is within it.

Speak words of Light. Let Light pour out of your mouth in cosmic syllables, like bubbles from a fish rising to the surface, going 'pop,' and spreading their essence, their pollen out into the universe.

Seed your universe with Light. So, it is."

The weekend after this meditation, my friend Sandy and I went to Mount Shasta. Over three days we hiked twenty miles around Lake Siskiyou and on the McCloud River with the three waterfalls.

We had one adventure where several times we lost the path around the lake. Twice we came to places where there were streams of water. For those, we were able to traverse rocks not laid out in a crossing path, but we made it across without getting wet.

Then we came to the Sacramento River, rushing and wide. Sandy decided to try her luck with rocks again. I watched her and couldn't see a path across. I entreated her to come back. We would keep looking.

In the near distance, we saw some logs that looked like they might go all the way across. We picked our way over to them. They did! There were three logs kind of tangled around each other.

Sandy walked across one roundish log that put her securely on the other side. She waved at me to come over.

I looked at that log and thought, *Nope*. My sneakers had no tread on them; they were meant for walking on even ground. I felt they were not going to keep me securely on the log. I considered taking them off to walk in bare feet.

But there was also another log a short distance into the river which could be reached after a brief traipse on the roundish log. This second one was much flatter and had been worn away so that the surface was uneven, with places where a slippery shoe sole could securely grip into and not slide off.

This second, flatter log reached the other side of the river at its roots. I ascertained that the roots were probably scalable without much trouble, and it looked like the ground was on the other side of the roots.

With all Sandy's entreaty for me to go the route of the round log, I set out on the flatter, probably redwood, tree.

Slowly, with focus on where I was stepping, and not on the rushing water below, I traversed the river.

All was well. We were successful! The rest of the ten-mile hike was a piece of cake.

I include this event because it seems to illustrate some of what Saint Germain was saying in my birthday meditation "Let the mountain sustain you. Let her enter your consciousness and lift you higher... This is the land of infinite possibilities... It's a land of peace..."

Meditation: 4-25-2021

I am in the golden dome of Melchizedek (a bright Light Being in charge of the universe as I discovered in my readings), at the center of the universe. I sit in his ascension seat (a vortex of energy that, in meditation, soaks into you, vibrating your energy at a rate closer to the energy of Source) and absorb his uplifting, golden light.

Metatron appears. I hear "Metatron's table." On the table are balls of radiating, luminous light—different colors, different sizes. I feel myself absorbing a ball of light and becoming more radiant, luminous. I hear, "You can be luminous wherever you are. You can glow."

I hear "Gift these balls." I give a ball to Diana, to Liam, to Brooke.

I notice that you can play with these balls. You can throw them as far as you want to, wherever you want to send Light. You can juggle them.

You can make Light designs in space with them. You can eat them, and the Light goes down your digestive tract, creating healing.

You can sit on them, and the Light goes up into you and through your body.

Their uses are infinite as Light is infinite. Joy abounds.

Spirit Leads; Life Expands

I began my master's degree in counseling in September of 1987. Our class had maybe fifteen people. We got to know each other intimately.

One class that stands out for me is group therapy, taught by a local psychologist. Besides having the didactic portion, our class became a group doing actual therapy.

Our teacher let the group develop as a group does, organically. We became vulnerable with each other and began to work on our issues.

During this class, I became acutely aware of my inner emotional struggles. I decided that I would begin my own therapy.

I thought I might work with our teacher and asked her how much she charged. It was too much for my budget, but she gave me the name of her colleague, Robert, whom she thought didn't charge as much.

I called him. The price was right. From the moment I sat down in his office, I felt comfortable. I began my individual therapy.

I stayed in therapy with him for sixteen years. I also participated in some of his groups.

Working with him was majorly life-changing for me. I was able to open places in my psyche that had been hidden from me my whole life—places of pain, sadness, depression, anger, and fear.

He held me in a compassionate space of understanding, creating clarity and healing as I gained the courage to release old patterns, to uncover what was hidden, to engage with as many parts of myself as I could. All to bring to light who I really am.

He said that for him, this work was Soul Making. I would rephrase that today to say, it is Soul Uncovering or Self Uncovering.

The work with Robert informed my life, my subsequent psychotherapy work, my choices, and my understanding of how and why people do what they do.

I learned that there are always reasons for people's thoughts, emotions, and behaviors and that if we can understand them, we can move to a place of empathy and understanding.

I attended grad school for two years. During that time, I also became friends with Sandra. She is a wise, smart, and compassionate woman who also has a great understanding of how people come to do what they do.

After our two years, Carly, Sandra, and I decided to celebrate with a backpacking trip to Desolation Wilderness in California.

Sandra had a cabin in nearby Strawberry, from which we could stay a night and leave early the next morning for Echo Lake, the beginning of our trek.

Our goal was Aloha Lake, some twelve miles in. We were carrying heavy packs with all our food, water, tents, and clothes for three days.

We traversed a lot of switchbacks that helped us climb out of the Echo Lake area and get to a flatter trail.

The three days were glorious. We were intrepid explorers! We came upon other smaller, pristine, clear lakes, saw chipmunks that kept us company, and felt peace, silence, and beauty as we fished and swam.

It was a wonderful present we gave ourselves for completing our two years. We sweated, got sore muscles, laughed, and enjoyed. It served as a tribute to an ending and a physical precursor demonstration for the next stage of our lives.

We had worked hard to get through the MA program and now we would have 3,600 hours of supervised therapy practice to conquer before we could take the state board exam for our licenses as MFTs (Marriage and Family Therapists).

We had fun while we persevered on our hike. And like our physical endurance exercise, we were up to the task of emerging victorious from this next task ahead of us.

It was Sandra who invited me to consider moving to the little house in Sacramento (when I parted from Jeremiah).

It was a perfect house for me. Two bedrooms, a fireplace, big front and back yards, and a side yard where I sometimes held parties. I lived there from 1988 to about 1996.

During this time while I was attending St Francis' Church and singing in the choir, I met some wonderful gay men: Luke, Thomas, and Caleb. Luke and Thomas were a couple at that time. We became friends and hung out many times over the years.

Thomas was in the Sacramento Ballet. He would get us comp tickets to see the shows. So fun! We watched him dance the Prince in *The Nutcracker* and multiple other roles. I enjoyed so much laughter, love, and sincere friendship with these guys.

Luke was a runner. In Yuba City, I had found out I was losing bone density. So, I started taking calcium and jogging. It strengthened my bones.

I had done a few 5Ks with a friend in respiratory therapy from Fremont hospital. He used to tell me about his woes with a former girlfriend who also worked in the hospital, but in the recovery room (where you go after surgery to wake up safely).

It may have been Luke who suggested we do some 5K runs. I had been doing three miles around my neighborhood in about thirty minutes. I was never a fast jogger. It was a good waker-upper for my day.

I was game.

I remember one run in the hills at Pollock Pines. The elevation there is about 4,000 feet. Sacramento is twenty-six feet. And Pollock Pines is in the Sierra Nevada Mountain range. I think I came in last in that 5K. Walking. I had no conditioning for altitude or up and down mountains.

But it was fun and beautiful and cold. I think my calves and quads took a week to recover.

Since I hadn't dated anyone since separating from Ron, Luke was always encouraging me. I had been scared. I had been so into Ron that it took a lot of work to heal my heart.

Jason sang in the choir at St Francis. He was a runner and did 5Ks. One Sunday, we chatted and ended up talking about the 5Ks. Luke and I invited him—or he invited himself—to join us in our runs.

Coming back from one race, Luke was driving his truck. I sat next to him in the middle, with Jason on the passenger side. Sometime on the way home, Jason put his hand on my leg. Luke noticed and I could feel him being surprised, as was I.

That was the beginning of a very short dating life with Jason.

It turned out Jason wasn't interested in committing to one person. I was of a different mind. I got attached to him but kept feeling his distance, even though we periodically went on dates.

In the winter, Luke and I thought it would be fun to go sledding somewhere up Interstate 80 near the ski resorts. We brought saucers and found a steep hill that was accommodating a profusion of sled goers—grown-ups, kids, and now, us.

We climbed to the top of the hill. It sure looked steep from up there. Luke said I should go first. He was nervous, I'm certain.

I got on my saucer and started down. Well, the saucer turned round and round, and finally had me going down backward as I lost control on what turned out to be a very icy hill.

Halfway down, I lost the saucer and continued down the hill headfirst on my back, bouncing all the way, over many icy bumps. At the bottom, I caught my breath and was actually able to stand up. I was shaken but could walk.

Luke came down to find me. So much for our sledding escapade. He was laughing, the stinker. He said it really did look funny watching my out-of-control bounces.

My right side was beginning to ache. Not long after that, I said I should probably go to the ER to get checked out.

We drove back to Sacramento and to one of the ERs. I had a cracked rib, not really broken, but not securely in one piece. They gave me Vicodin and said it would heal. They said they didn't tape the ribs anymore.

I went home to my little house and began to live on the couch. It was hard to take a deep breath. The Vicodin tore up my stomach with pain even worse than the rib.

I called my acupuncturist. He did tape me up. That was outstanding. It relieved the pain, and I could breathe and move around, albeit gingerly. I know it helped hasten the healing.

During this time of necessary rest, I still had a connection with Jason, though it was pretty tenuous. He called and said he wanted to come over to see how I was doing.

He came with a new woman he was dating. The conversation was stunningly short. I was shocked and hurt that he would bring over the Other Woman! I ushered them out within five minutes.

Later, Jason was able to meet me for a snack while I told my side of the story. I give him credit that he sat and listened and appeared to understand and was sorry.

I was glad that I spoke up for myself and that, even if he didn't tune in to the pain he was creating at the time, he was able to hear me. I was practicing speaking my truth.

Speaking up for myself was something I had to learn over time. I didn't observe my mom doing that. She was quiet and seemed to go along with my dad on most things.

Growing up, we were not really encouraged to speak about negative feelings we had, like anger or sadness. Those went deep within. My therapy was helping to unleash them.

Another thing that I am grateful to Jason for is that his behavior on that day burst open a door to my anger. For two straight months after his visit to my little house, I was enraged. I would wake up at 2 a.m., flaming mad and wanting to lash out.

I worked this in therapy. I worked it at home. I would take a large pad of artist's paper and crayons and, without thinking about it, draw whatever came out of my body through my arm and hand. I let the feeling emerge on the paper. All abstract. Different colors and shapes. Page after page, until I felt done with that outpouring.

I would journal in the same fashion. No editing, just writing whatever showed up in my awareness; all the ugly, angry, no-holds-barred images and feelings. I had some very creative, destructive ideas as I worked to release my anger.

At that time, I worked at a small, county-funded agency of social workers and therapists in training. Here, I was getting some of my 3,600 supervised hours.

We would get calls from family members or neighbors of folks aged fifty-five and over. The calls were from concerned people who thought our potential client was not doing well at all and needed to be checked out.

We would go to the person's house, and, for some unknown reason, they always let us in to do a psychological evaluation.

 If they were a danger to themselves or others or were gravely disabled (couldn't take care of themselves safely), we would write a 5150, (a legal document that can be written by a nurse, doctor, or other trained health professional to involuntarily detain someone for seventy-two hours), call the police or ambulance, and transport them to a psychiatric hospital or an ER.

During one office phone call, I was on the phone with Jason's ex-wife. She had been mad at me because I was dating Jason. I felt she had no reason to be jealous because she wasn't married to him anymore! I found my anger surging. I imagined a very ingenious (or so I thought) way of torturing her. But of course, I never acted on it.

Later I told my office mates and they, knowing that I was going through an intense therapeutic anger purge, understood but joked that they wouldn't want to get on my bad side!

At the time, I was also in a therapy consult group with my therapist's teacher. He is awesome and was always researching cutting-edge therapy treatment.

I remember him saying, "We need to claim our own rage, hate, and desire to do damage. Then, when we work through it, we won't act it out."

And, also, "There are two types of anger, connected and unconnected. If you are connected to your anger (or hate), you can claim it and work with it to not act it out. If you are unconnected to your anger, you are more likely to act it out and hurt someone or something, because it is in you and alive and is an intense energy that wants to go somewhere."

During those two months, I connected to my rage and was working it, I also got connected to my intense pain and hurt underneath the anger. This was what was really fueling the fury. In my hurt, I felt helpless because I couldn't make it go away. I wanted to do something about it, but I felt trapped in it. Feeling anger gave me a sense of power and that seemed more bearable than the feelings of hurt and helplessness.

Many clients and some friends have attested to this experience also.

Do you have unresolved anger or pain that can be worked so it doesn't affect your life? There are many styles of releasing pent-up emotions: art, journaling, EFT (tapping), and EMDR, for instance.

Meditation: 5-2-2021

Deep feeling of being connected to Source. I hear Source say, "My thoughts are your thoughts." It's a strong, filling energy. It's beyond all color or shape. Pure, luminous Light. It's for me to be connected to this now, in all moments. To live my life in at-onement with Source and to realize how I am of Source.

Meditation: 5-3-2021

Source says, "Stay with Me. Abide with Me. Watch and pray. Watch and pray." Words from a song from Taizé, a simple musical chanting prayer in the Catholic Church.

Asking to clear my fear of complete surrender, aware of wanting to control, out of not trusting—a long experience of that—feeling the sweet, crystal-clear Light of Source, and being immersed in the cleansing, reassuring Light and Love. I hear, "Surrender to Me." I feel my mind being wary as I also feel the reassuring Light.

"My thoughts are your thoughts." I ask for assistance in this.

In the start of meditation, I feel Emmanuel (a name meaning "God with Us") appearing with love to support me.

"I have created you. In Me you are created. And you are you."

36

In the Spirit of Love, There is Sacred Work and Play

Besides working for the county agency, which was my living wage job, I also worked at Family Service Agency getting hours as an MFT intern. They paid $10 per hour.

I got the best training for being a therapist there. We saw individuals, kids, and couples.

I had a great supervisor. We had monthly staff meetings where we attended trainings on relevant topics.

Another job where I received supervised intern hours was at the county mental hospital. I worked as an RN in the crisis unit. There, I was exposed to intense anger from others and got practice staying balanced as clients acted out.

People were brought in on 5150s for being suicidal, homicidal, or gravely disabled (unable to care for themselves). Some had OD'd on pills and the ER of a hospital had cleared them for further mental health treatment. Some were high on methamphetamines or other drugs. Some were violent.

With the violent ones, we sometimes needed to do what we called "take-downs." This was not my favorite!

A good number of staff would surround the person who was trying to do damage. Then, each staff member would take hold of a limb or part of the torso and carry them to a cot in an isolation room. While they were still being held down, I, as the nurse, gave them what was referred to as "the cocktail," three shots to help their out-of-control system stabilize.

Most of the time, the cocktail worked. They went to sleep and woke up calm and a bit clearer.

I remember one time when a developmentally disabled, non-English speaking Russian woman probably in her thirties was brought in. She had been living with her family and they were no longer able to contain her. She was quite psychotic.

I gave her the cocktail. It didn't touch her. No effect.

These were potent drugs—an anti-psychotic, a sedative, and a drug to counter the side effects of antipsychotics. I seem to recall that we couldn't give her more drugs because we would have to wait a certain number of hours before it was safe. We could only contain her in a room.

I gained a lot on this job.

One thing I gained was the wonderful feeling of working with a tightly knit team. I appreciated all the staff and their sense of dedication to the work, of responsibility to the clients, and of responsibility to each other.

I was struck by the love they had for people and their ability to rise to each crisis immediately, with clear intent, good boundaries, and appropriate behavior. We supported each other. We had to. Our safety and the clients' safety depended on it.

Besides keeping people safe, each of us took a turn in doing a psychological evaluation of each incoming client. Part of this process was doing a diagnosis according to the DSM (*Diagnostic and Statistical Manual*, the reference book that mental health professionals use to assign a diagnosis to a person's struggle).

Working at this clinic, I learned something about practically every diagnosis in the DSM. This was to help me later when I needed to assign a diagnosis for insurance payments in private practice.

As the RN on the team, I did the initial medical evaluation for every client who arrived. I took their blood pressure, pulse, and respiration, and asked them a few questions about their meds and health.

This was undeniably a learn-on-the-job situation in every way.

Once a twenty- or thirty-something developmentally disabled woman came in. She sat down in the chair for me to take her blood pressure.

To try and connect with her, I leaned down at eye level with her. She punched me in the nose. Ouch! That hurt! She landed a good one. I didn't think it was broken, but that was a lesson learned.

I also learned that folks who were paranoid needed to not feel boxed in. That meant that when we were sitting with them in a closed-up, small room doing the evaluation, they needed to have the door in sight and accessible, if for no other reason than to feel visually that they had some control.

We also needed to consider our own safety and evaluate how to position ourselves in case we needed to exit quickly.

I learned to speak very non-judgmentally, objectively, but firmly when asking questions of our struggling clients.

I loved these staff members. We would get together outside of work for potlucks at someone's house. Super Bowl Sunday was a big deal for everyone but me. (I never was into football.)

But I went to the party because these people also knew how to enjoy each other and have a good time. There was a lot of joking around and kidding each other.

Because we worked so closely together and these folks were quite astute at reading people (a lot of practice on the job!), we knew each other well. All our foibles, fears, and strengths were acknowledged—and fair game!

And there was a lot of celebrating when each person had success, as well as empathy and support when each of us had our own struggles.

It wasn't perfect, but what is?! But, as I dwell on groups I've been in, I am grateful for these big-hearted folks who worked so hard in a very challenging setting.

Thinking back to the group I worked with in my other county agency, where we visited folks in their homes, I have fond memories of those folks also.

We were maybe five or six people in a small office. These folks were also dedicated to the work. They were able to have fun together and really liked each other.

I remember one goofy time when a staff person had a birthday. Often, she was the voice of clarity and reason in an untenable situation. She acted as a reality check in the agency. She was very good at reading people and a comedian besides. She had a knack for creating droll, witty jokes.

A few of us decided we needed to outdo her cleverness. We blew up and cut out a picture of her face to be the normal size of her head, then stole some of her clothes that were stashed in her office.

We found a mannequin somewhere (don't ask me how). We dressed it in her clothes and pasted the blown-up face cut-out on its head, then seated this doppelganger in her office chair.

We put a birthday cake in front of her office twin, with, of course, too many candles on the cake.

She came in the next day on her birthday and, to our great delight had the perfect response! To witness the surprise on her face was quite sufficient to satisfy our need to pull one over on her. And I do believe, she probably wasn't quite sure how to take our affection for her.

Our boss at this agency was the one signing off on my supervised intern hours. She was great, with a big heart. She was smart, a go-getter, super supportive, and direct. We would gather at her house for parties. She set up our birthday lunches at local restaurants.

Since this agency needed a case manager, she asked if I wanted to have that position. I thought, *Sure, why not?* I could surely figure out how to do that. (Didn't that seem to be my schtick, creating a job where there had been none?)

So, I set about learning what that entailed and created a structure for the case management position. Then I became the case manager.

This job showed me another aspect of mental health: the contributing home environment, how the police were needed, and more on the varying psychiatric hospitals.

When we went to a person's home to evaluate their mental state and decided they needed a 5150, we most often had to call the police to transport the client to an ER or psychiatric hospital.

Because we were there and could explain the situation to the police, for the most part, things went smoothly. I'm not recalling any difficult scenes.

Or we might decide that the person needed case management instead of hospitalization. That was my job to follow up, find resources for them, and connect them with the help they needed.

Besides getting more intern hours for my MFT license, I worked in a supportive environment with dedicated, heart-centered people. And I, once again, learned about creating something where there had been nothing.

Another job that provided me with intern hours was at a psychiatric hospital in Fairfield, CA. It has since closed. I worked in the intake department, evaluating people mainly for hospitalization.

At that time, one of the psychiatrists was Daniel Amen (before he was famous). He was studying ADHD and had us give kids' parents questionnaires about their child that were designed to determine if the child had ADHD.

He went on to write books about the brain, do workshops, and study the brain using SPECT scans, which look at the metabolism of the brain versus the structure, which is what CTs and MRIs do.

Using the SPECT scan, he and his team can pinpoint the areas that are damaged, underactive, and overactive, and from that, advise treatment. He favors natural treatments first but prescribes meds if that is called for.

I always remember his statement at a workshop I attended: "Psychiatrists are the only doctors who don't look at the organ they are treating." SPECT scans may still not be paid for by insurance, so psychiatrists need to diagnose from symptoms and reports from others.

I was grateful for my time at Solano Park Hospital. The staff I worked with were also heart-centered people and we became friends.

But driving an hour each way to work got to be old, even though traffic going and coming was light. I worked the evening shift, 3 p.m. to 11 p.m., and missed rush hour each way. It just wasn't my dream job.

I stayed the longest at the Family Service Agency job, from 1991 to 1995. I am very grateful for the training I received there. I learned a lot about doing therapy with folks.

37

Love Takes a Stand

In the spring of 1992, I attended a three-day conference of the CAMFT (California Association of Marriage and Family Therapists) in LA with a fellow therapist intern, Elena.

This was the time on April 29, 1992, when four Los Angeles policemen were acquitted of the beating of Rodney King, an African American man, even though King had skull fractures, broken bones and teeth, and permanent brain damage.

Three hours after the acquittal, LA, having endured years of racial injustice in the city, erupted in rage – five days of rioting including looting, fires, property damage, and beatings of light-skinned people. 1,000 buildings were damaged, and 2,000 businesses were destroyed. There were fifty deaths and $1 billion in damage.

Elena and I had debated whether it was prudent to go to LA then. The conference was at the airport hotel and was going ahead, despite some fear that it might be canceled due to the unrest. We decided it was important we go. We wanted to lend some local supportive energy to our belief in equal rights for all. We would do it.

As it turned out, none of the violence reached the airport hotel where the conference was held. The conference supportively addressed what was going on with the folks who were outraged. They talked about helping folks with their anger in a therapy situation, in order to heal from pain and rage, and proactively, constructively, deal with helplessness, abuse, hate, etc. We were then able to go ahead with focusing on the conference.

38

Venturing Out Again to Earth Relationship

My therapist had been encouraging me to get out there and date. It had been quite a few years since my breakup with Ron and I had been scared to get hurt again (my brief encounter with Jason notwithstanding). But my therapist worked with me and kept saying, "Feel your longing! Feel your longing!" I thought, *Okay, I will!*

The first night at the conference, they held a dance. Well, I love to dance—most especially my way. If I like it, I feel the music in my body and I let my body do its thing. I feel the rhythm of the beat and jump, stomp, slide, wiggle, and throw my arms around. I go with the flow. If the music moves me, I can keep dancing all night.

Well, they had good music that night. I was feeling it. Movin' and groovin'. One guy noticed me. Maybe I was also "feeling my longing."

But he wasn't particularly interesting to me. After dancing, I went to bed.

The next day in between workshops, I went swimming in the hotel pool. I attracted the attention of another guy, mostly from a distance. That connection was basically a bust.

In between workshops, I was taking a break, sitting on a comfy chair next to another comfy chair. A guy saw me and sat down next to me.

We chatted. It turned out he was one of the conference's organizers. He was also an intern, like me, and his work focused on men's groups and men's issues. I thought that was cool.

A kind of intense energy developed between us—electric. Sometime in our conversation, he was very unconsciously making motions with his hands. One hand made a circle while the other, with one finger, bounced in and out of the circle over and over. I noticed. I don't think he did. (I must have been feeling my longing!)

He invited me to sit with him and his cohorts at breakfast the next morning, which I did. Again, there was a very strong, palpable electric energy between us.

This was the last morning of the event. We exchanged phone numbers and addresses and he promised to come to visit me in Sacramento. (He lived in LA.) I hoped he would. He never got in touch. It was a short-lived connection. I was sad for a while.

Meditation: 5-23-2021 "When you struggle, Source will support you"

Feeling the loneliness. JG (intuitive reader) says it's because I don't have folks around that are as spiritually evolved as me. Well, maybe. But today in meditation and for the last few days, I've been working to find the clear cause and effect of this feeling that has come up to be looked at.

I brought in the spiritual clearing tools I know—the Violet Flame, core fear matrix removal program, cosmic fire (matchstick size, at the base of my spine), wind clearing device of the Arcturians, and the platinum net of Metatron.

I invited in all the wonderful spiritual guides who help facilitate these tools: Vywamus (a Galactic Light Being), the Arcturians (a community of Christ-centered Light folks), Michael and Faith (the Archangels), Raphael and Mother Mary, Holy Amethyst and Zadkiel, Metatron, the Ascended Ones (like Jesus), Saint Germain, El Morya, Djwahl Kuhl, Melchizedek, the Multi-Universal Logos, the council of twelve close to the heart of the Divine, and all the Angels of Light who also help us. These are those who occurred to me today.

Your Lineage Informs and Supports Your Earth Experiences

What showed up for me with this last meditation was my mother this lifetime. She was, and remains, a mystery. She was very smart, had talents in many areas, and worked for equal rights for all.

She was agoraphobic when I was born. And suicidal (postpartum depression?). She wrote a letter to my dad, who was doing his PhD in Delaware while she stayed with his mom in New York City. In it, she said she could easily drive her car off a bridge.

She was a quiet woman. Growing up, we barely heard her talk about much. My dad held the floor in that department, and she seemed content to let him dominate verbally.

I'm not sure when it began, but she criticized her daughters—me and my younger sister, Liza. Once the extended family was having dinner at a restaurant and suddenly, apropos of nothing, my mom let fly, "Liza is such a mouse!" There was dead silence at the table. No one knew what to say to that. Then, I believe, the conversation just went on as if that hadn't happened.

Once when she came to visit with me and my new baby, she said, "I wonder why his grandma is so much better at soothing him than his mother." I didn't grace that with a response. I thought about it though and realized that it actually wasn't true. She really wasn't more able to calm him down.

When I was about fifteen years old (my brother would have been twelve and my sister nine), my parents went on a trip. My mom's mother, Grandma, came to take care of us. One day, while we were sitting in the living room, Grandma made a comment to me I never forgot. She said she was always worried for us kids because we had a mom like her daughter. She didn't elaborate, but she had real concern for us.

My mom was always awkward around people. Besides her cutting remarks toward her daughters, which happened regularly, she would make off-the-wall comments in conversation that didn't seem to relate to anything. My dad was always filling in the blanks for her, explaining what she really meant.

Some of my therapy work was to help heal the repeated feeling of the knife-like jab that went to my heart from her criticism. I know my sister had similar experiences.

As I progressed in my therapy healing, I noticed more clearly that my mom saw the world very differently from most people. She interpreted events as negative that weren't. When she stated how awful things were, she cast a pall on the atmosphere. As I grew more into my own power, I set boundaries with her, saying, "No mom, it isn't like that. It's like this." It surprised her, I think, because she backed down.

Some of me wonders if she was frustrated by not manifesting more of her creative juices—her excellent writing, for instance. My niece, my brother's daughter, once said to me that she wondered if Grandma was a product of the patriarchy. And, as I consider all this, I think this is definitely part of my mom's story.

And as I write this, my brother texts me reminding me that my mom's parents were cold and distant with their three kids. My grandma was highly anxious besides.

My mom told of a time when she was a kid upstairs in their house. My granddad had gone to visit a lady friend who needed some help.

He came home and my mom heard this unearthly wail from her mom on the first floor. She said it was like an animal in excruciating pain. Perhaps it was my grandma's insecurity, which would have begun in her childhood.

My grandma's parents were German and alcoholic. Her father died and her mother remarried a good man.

Apparently, my great grandma was mean to her two girls. My mom told me a story where great grandma was on the couch downstairs, hungover. Her eldest daughter, Helen, my grandma Marie's sister, was very sick upstairs with the flu.

My Grandma Marie told her mother that her sister, Helen, was so hot! Great Grandma just yelled at her. Grandma got Helen some water and crept quietly up the stairs so as not to be noticed by her mother.

That amount of stress and lack of mothering would help account for my grandma's anxiety. It also helps to explain why Grandma had insecure attachment issues, hence her panic when her husband went to see another woman, even if just to help her.

We inherit patterns, tendencies, and struggles from all the generations that came before us. These show up in our DNA, our psychology, and our body styles. So, we not only have our own lifetime of experiences, but we also have our relatives' life histories that influence us.

Knowing this, I wonder how come my great grandparents drank. What stress were they under? What were their lives like? Why was great grandma so disconnected from her children? What aspect of this was passed down to her daughter, my grandma, and then to my own mother?

We may never know the facts of our ancestors, but we can notice if some of their dysfunctional behavior, mindsets, and feelings made their way into our organism or relationships. We can then work to create healing and change our lives for the better.

We Are Products of Our Ancestors and Society

My dad had a more dominant personality than my mother. We know that in all our recorded history, men have always been more dominant than women and this could have been one reason, along with his typically Aquarius penchant for talking, that he tended to dominate in their relationship.

Even though my dad's parents were free thinkers—creative, bohemian, artists—they were also subject to the influence of the seemingly universal dominance of men, even if unconsciously.

My Russian grandparents had a hard time getting pregnant, so when they did conceive, they called my dad the miracle child. I wonder if this energy influenced how my dad saw himself.

Certainly, on the surface, he didn't look egoistic. But he always seemed to like an audience.

In his later years when I would go visit him and my mother in New Jersey, he wanted to keep talking long past my bedtime. I would say, "I'm tired. Have to go to bed now, Dad." But he would keep talking. Even as I went up the steps to the bedroom, he kept talking.

Once I was having a chat with him when Mom came into the room to tell us something. He was quite annoyed with her for interrupting him. "Can't you see I'm talking?"

Mom undoubtedly had a lot to overcome; tendencies and patterns passed down most likely even before the influences of her grandmother, not to mention her own life experiences.

We can help release and heal these intergenerational imprints if we choose.

Meditation: 5-24-2021

I invite in my normal inter-dimensional support system. The energy keeps building and becomes very powerful.

My son drops something in the kitchen. A loud crash. I hear it but it doesn't disturb my meditation. I am in deep.

I feel and see Jesus in my mind's eye. I feel the Light entering all parts of me—mind, heart, and body, weaving connections so that all is linked in order that I work as one being.

I get the feeling that as I become more embodied Light, that energy will ooze out of my skin and affect those around me. I hear advice, "Let the Light in, receive, surrender."

The past few days I have been clearing the blocks that have shown up. As I type this, I hear, "Yes." I have been clearing the way for more Light to dwell within me.

If the fact that that crash in the kitchen during meditation didn't disturb my peace is any indication, this process could lead to existing in the "peace that passeth all understanding".

I have noticed that the more I meditate, the more peaceful I have become in general. Even yesterday, the workers outside my house were drilling holes in the road. The noise was tremendous. It didn't affect my meditation.

This is not to say that I'm always cool, calm, and collected! But I notice a definite shift in my equilibrium; stuff doesn't knock me off center as easily. So far!

A Goal Reached

I devoted myself to finishing my intern hours.

By the end of 1992, I had all my 3,600 hours and applied to the state to take the licensing exam.

First came the multiple choice. If you passed that, you went on to the practical. I studied and studied using materials created for that purpose. I took a lot of practice exams.

I was ready. I took the written exam in a big room with lots of tables laid out. There were a lot of people taking it at the same time The rules were fierce to keep people from cheating.

We had to wait over a month before we knew if we passed. I passed!

On to the practical. For this part, we went to a hotel at the San Francisco airport. We would be sitting in one of the hotel rooms with two examiners. This was the scary one.

I got more study materials and found a study partner, and we practiced and practiced. For the test, we would be given a vignette of an imagined client. We had to analyze it thoroughly. We were timed.

There was a lot of material we had to cover. They would be recording it. People often took this test two, three, or more times. Part of the dilemma was nerves; folks couldn't think clearly.

The day came. Eek! The night before, I relaxed, as was advised. I got up early and drove to the San Francisco airport hotel. I parked, found where I was supposed to go, and signed in. Then I waited until they were ready for me.

It was pretty freaky all around. When it was my turn, I went up in the elevator to maybe the ninth floor and found the room number.

I went in and saw the two examiners. There was a rectangular table set up with a recorder. They sat on one side; I was directed to sit opposite them.

Each section of the test was timed. I had maybe two or three minutes to read the vignette, make notes, and come up with my diagnosis and plan.

They were going to rate me on whether I was a safe therapist and covered the essential points about symptoms, possible diagnosis, problems to deal with, type of approach, and overall plan.

After three or so minutes of initial analysis, I had to start talking. Okay, gulp, deep breath.

The whole thing was maybe ten to fifteen minutes. Should I make eye contact with them? I did.

One of them especially seemed friendly, but what did that really mean? I was processing this as I was also trying to be smart and concise and include all the talking points.

They said, "Time's up," and that was that. I left, drove home, and waited for some weeks. This was in March or April of 1993.

The letter came from the BBS (the state board that decides these things) in the summer. We wanted to get a big letter—that one had our license in it. A small letter was, "Oh, no! Try again."

It was a big letter! I passed and I got my license. Wow. The long five-and-a-half-year journey was complete. I did it! And, once again, I was so grateful. I had passed on the first go-round. Whew!

I had had so much support, had met so many wonderful people along the way, had learned a whole new way of thinking about people, and had grown immensely within myself.

Celebration time! My case management job with the county program had a party, my therapist was elated, and folks at Family Service Agency applauded.

The Dance of the Divine
Feminine on Earth

During the time I was waiting to hear about my results, I decided it was time to date again. I was done focusing on the MFT preparation, so I had energy and could move in other directions.

I heard that there was a weekly Contra dance event and decided that I would try that out as I ventured out into the dating world again. The first dance was fun and good exercise. Contra dance incorporates styles from seventeenth-century Scottish, English, and French dances, as well as some Appalachian and African influences into big group line dances. I found that the sequence entailed having multiple partners even for one dance. That was cool because you got to check out a bunch of guys. Everyone asked each other to dance. It was pretty chill.

By the time I went to a second dance, I was learning more of the steps. They had a caller who taught you all the steps for each dance before it began for real. There was a banjo, a fiddle, and a guitar to keep the energy moving.

Meditation 5-11-2021 Support from My Female Ancestors

I feel my mothers over the generations, back through the millennia, all in a long chain, connected, linked to each other, and supporting me. Thousands of women who gave birth to me and it all links back to Divine Mother holding us all, infusing us with her essence, the energy of birth, creation, and the Divine Feminine. All these women gifting me with their gifts, saying, "We are here for you."

I relax to receive. I feel Divine Mother intending this sequence to gift all her children. We can receive all the gifts of our lineage as we get quiet, relax, and lose control. They are all there, waiting to love us each in their way.

We can receive. We are here to express all these aspects of us, all seeds existing in our body, in our mind, in our heart, in our spirit, waiting to be activated by our willingness, saying yes. Say yes, now. I love you.

The third time I went to the Contra Dance, they had the live band, the caller, and the dances where you changed partners a lot. For one dance, I was positioned at the end of one of the two lines, ready to dance in when it was my turn.

Next to me at the end of the other line was a dude. We were to hold hands and begin to dance down the lines. When our hands touched, my right to his left, an electric spark passed between us—not visibly, but definitely felt.

I looked at him more closely. I thought he looked a bit sad, but I could tell he felt the fire too. An energy was building between us. No words had been spoken. It was hard to hear over the band!

Later when we finished dancing, he sought me out and introduced himself. David was his name. He asked if I wanted to get coffee and a snack. Some other people from the dance were meeting at the Tower Cafe. I said yes and drove over with him in his car.

Of course, I didn't have coffee—I'd be awake all night. As we chatted, I thought he was an interesting fellow, intelligent and talking about subjects that I was partial to.

He drove me back to my car. He was very interested to see what kind of car I drove—a Honda.

I could tell he was flustered. He was sitting in my passenger seat and bumped his head on the car roof getting out. He asked me for my phone number and gave me his, then suggested we go out on a date.

He left my phone number in my car.

So, I called him to ask about that date. He suggested we go out to dinner at a Thai restaurant. I said yes and gave him my phone number again.

The date was awkward. Conversation was broken up by silences. I found myself trying to fill in the spaces.

We went on more dates and some of the floundering connection attempts dissipated. He came over one day, and we sat on my couch each on an end but facing each other. I felt him settle into listening and I liked it.

I was also going to St. Francis Church then and I wanted him to go with me. He did, but it wasn't really his thing. I appreciated that he went.

I had some doubts about this burgeoning relationship. For one, he smoked, and I couldn't stand cigarette smoke. At one point when we were farther along, when we were hanging out, I asked him to wash his face and hands each time he smoked. He did.

But the smell was still on his clothes. After a while, he decided that he would quit. He had been smoking for many years. I suggested he get some acupuncture or some aid to help him. He said he was just going to quit.

He did. He made up his mind and did it. He never went back. That was impressive.

It was April of 1993 when I met David, when I was waiting for my MFT license results. Seemed like a great time to celebrate!

We thought that going to Hawaii would be amazing. My dad gifted me with the trip. So sweet.

We went for ten days to Kauai and the Big Island. Because we knew that food was expensive there and we had booked a condo where we could cook, we filled a suitcase with dry food, beans, rice, etc. (In those days there wasn't such onboard luggage scrutiny.)

We went first to Hawaii Island. We had a gorgeous hike among giant ferns and lava beds in the Kilauea Caldera. We went to the beach in Hilo and drove around to Kona.

Then we flew to Kauai. That was the best! We stayed in a condo in Princeville, right above a sweet little beach. We snorkeled with colorful fish. I saw a sand shark below me, just swimming, chill. David saw sea turtles.

We hiked up to the top of the Na Pali coast (breathtaking!) to a trail that led inland to a waterfall. Other hikers kept us on the path.

We snorkeled more at Poipu on a supremely windy day.

We hiked in Waimea canyon, which was outstanding. The flowers and other foliage were exquisite.

We did our version of a luau at a diner that served roast pig and poi and a sweet cake for dessert.

We bathed in the soothing, colorful music of traditional Hawaii, listening to the tapes as we drove to new adventures on the island.

In all my years with David, I never saw him more relaxed than when we were in Hawaii. He was like a little kid, playful and happy. No stress.

We returned to the mainland refreshed.

In the summer I received my license! Whoo-hoo! I continued to work at the Family Service Agency and the county program.

I considered what I really wanted to do now that I had my license to practice psychotherapy. I determined that I would start a private practice.

So, I did. In 1994, I opened an office in a suite with two other therapists inside a bigger office building. I had two clients.

After a time, about 1995, not feeling that the office building vibe was my style, I started looking for another office in a house. I found one owned by two lovely gentlemen who were also therapists. They owned and managed two houses, all for therapists. I moved into a small room that could fit me and a client.

I stayed in this space for a few years, moving into a larger office when it became available. This second room was big enough to hold groups.

When I opened my practice, I signed up with health insurance companies to increase my client base. I did my own billing and managed all parts of the business.

My practice began to grow as I got insurance referrals. I contracted with the Area 4 Agency on Aging to counsel and support caregivers of older adults. They paid me $50 per hour for a limited number of sessions—quite a step up from $10 per hour at Family Service Agency!

I moved into leading therapy groups. I really liked the group interaction—how each person added their uniqueness to the whole, how each individual perspective helped the others see things differently, and how, as one person gained courage and became vulnerable, it emboldened others to do the same.

The groups had rules, like if you were triggered (felt angry, sad) by someone, you spoke about it in the first person: "When you said this, I felt this." This way, folks learned to take responsibility for their feelings and not blame the other.

Another rule: What is said in the group, stays in the group; no talking about group content outside.

And: No out-of-group relationships; they create subgroups within the whole and subvert the group dynamic and feeling of safety.

Some of my groups went on for years—people left; new people joined.

I always enjoyed the group work. These were previews of later workshops that I would create.

My individual practice began to grow. Some clients became long-term—they wanted to work on issues that required slow, steady unraveling and subsequent integration into a new way of being.

I began to get referrals from doctors or former and present clients, in addition to insurance referrals.

My relationship with David was also progressing. I continued to have questions (maybe who doesn't?) but I brought my concerns to my therapy and that seemed to resolve them for the moment.

We moved in together in his house. It was a sweet little house, the first he ever bought. We were thinking that someday we would get married.

You Encounter Source by Following Your True Nature

I began to feel that I wanted a child. David didn't. He said he didn't think he would be a good dad. His parents had divorced, and it hadn't been pretty.

My feeling persisted, so David agreed to come to therapy with me to sort out his doubts about fatherhood.

After a time of processing, David decided he could go for it.

We began trying to get pregnant but were not successful. My gynecologist said she would help me get pregnant—I was forty-seven. She wasn't worried about old eggs or about my body being older. She said I was healthy. And so, I would have gone for it.

But David was concerned about me being pregnant at forty-seven. He thought my body wouldn't be able to take it. He thought we could adopt. Since he had agreed to be a dad after so much inner work, I decided I wouldn't argue the issue and said we could go ahead with adoption.

So, I began looking for adoption agencies. We interviewed five or six folks, including lawyers who served as adoption liaisons. We finally settled on a small agency run by one woman and her team.

She seemed to have experience and good reviews and we felt we could work with her.

Now we needed to put together our life book—a compilation of pictures and text that told about us. This would be read by prospective birth moms to see if they were drawn to us.

That took quite a bit of work! We wanted to point out our good qualities, of course!

Madeline, the adoption coordinator, also helped the parents-to-be prepare with classes and support groups. We attended several meetings where folks talked about their fears, their hopes, and their experiences waiting for their own birth mothers.

David and I were not married but were planning on it. Madeline said that it would help our adoption chances if we were married. We were going to be married but we were planning on spring of 1997. This was the fall of 1996. We thought, *Why not get married now?*

So, we did, on September 13, 1996, at the justice of the peace. We had a few friends attend. It was kind of a riot. We stood under a trellis with fake flowers woven through the latticework.

The officiant was Latina with a heavy accent, so it was hard to understand her. We repeated after her as she spoke the magic words.

Then it came time for the rings. We had none. Our friends let us borrow their rings, and she pronounced us man and wife. Whew! Crazy. It was the first time for both of us.

I remember in my early twenties thinking that I would marry later in life. And here it was coming true!

We had reservations for lunch with our friends at a restaurant in Old Sacramento on the waterfront. We had a blast. Our friends were so loving and celebratory. It was a good wedding.

We had a weekend honeymoon in a quaint town toward the coast, and then came home to wait for our birth mother. Over the next months, we met with several pregnant women who were looking for adoptive parents. We had been told that when the right person showed up both they and we would know it.

Of course, lots of people wanted to adopt a baby, but we were willing to wait.

As the months went on, I started planning our real marriage celebration, which was scheduled for April of 1997.

I had a ball planning it. I wanted it to reflect our values diversity, and the inclusion of many cultural traditions. I researched marriage ceremonies across the globe and picked out ones that felt like us and that spoke to our feelings.

I also wanted our friends to participate, not just be observers.

Of course, most of you know the work involved: the caterer, the venue, the helpers, the gift registry, and so much more.

We didn't want our parents to pay for this. We would foot the bill. All our friends helped.

I found a caterer that seemed perfect. They would deliver and set up the food, but not serve it. My dear friend Carly and her sisters helped with that.

I found a wedding cake at a noted local bakery that made the best pastries.

I was going to St. Francis Church at that time, and one of the priests, Father Adam, agreed to come and bless our celebration. He was basically the officiant without doing the regular marriage ceremony.

In Spirit, You Do It
Your Way!

We didn't want to hold our marriage blessing ceremony in a church. David wasn't into churches, having grown up in a conservative Christian congregation.

He said he was still recovering and sorting out the rigid dogma that had settled into his consciousness. One thing I liked about him was how he questioned. If it didn't feel right, he investigated.

My friend Caroline lived in a community that had an outdoor gazebo situated on a good-sized lawn. We were able to rent that space plus their rec center for the day.

Our friends were all excited to be participants in our party. I put together maybe five to eight wedding prayers from different cultures and gave one to each friend. At a designated time, each person would stand up and read their prayer out loud to everyone.

I found a Native American story about marriage and my dear friend Elizabeth, the actress, agreed to tell it. She also has a magnificent voice and sang one of the songs I picked out.

Some of my musical friends volunteered to sing other musical pieces about Love and Spirit, with alto, soprano, tenor, and bass sections!

My sister and her partner brought their three little girls to be flower girls.

Both of our families came to be with us.

David wanted us to play a guitar piece in the ceremony. We found a song we both liked a lot, with two parts. He would do the lead and I, the backup. He is a good guitarist, but I had taught myself only basic chords.

This piece had chords I had never seen. They required finger stretches and changes that challenged my small hands. We were able to have a musical friend change the key, but the chording was still difficult for me.

At times, I wanted to give up on the practice, but I persisted. By the day of the celebration, I had pretty much made it work.

The time came for our duet. We got our guitars and David began to tune them to each other. He was so nervous that he could barely focus.

This extremely engaging part of the event went on for probably not more than five to ten minutes, but to all of us, it seemed an eternity!

During these embarrassing moments, Father Adam came to our rescue, "This is their practice for the coming years!" The laughter buoyed us all through the moment.

And we pulled it off! We were proud of ourselves.

We had also written vows for each other, which we read.

Father Adam told the story of the velveteen rabbit, so perfect and fitting, about becoming real.

Then it was time to party!

Caroline and her sisters, Mia and Olivia, were devoted, tireless servers who kept the party food replenished.

We had a DJ who didn't always play the music we had asked for, but the joyful mood of the crowd remained undiminished.

Someone had the bright idea to start a snake dance, where one person started a line in time to the music. We held hands in a line and weaved in, though, and around each other.

The toasts were loving and sweet, from my brother and father, David's stepdad, and others.

We did the traditional wedding cake feed-each-other thing too.

Apparently, we didn't have enough food because my brother told me later that he was starving, and my dad took a few of them out for seafood.

The celebration was a success. Afterward, everyone helped clean up. David and I had spent about $2,000 in total.

People told us later it was the most fun wedding they had ever been to.

The next day, of course, we opened wedding presents.

We did a longer honeymoon than the first, in the Carmel area. We rode bikes, went to the beach, and had a relaxing time for a few days.

45

The Divine Wants You to be Happy!

When we got back to Sacramento, we got a phone call from our adoption facilitator, Madeline, who said there was a young lady who wanted to meet us.

I had wondered if our ages would deter potential birth moms; David was forty-three, and I was forty-nine.

I hoped this meeting would go well. The other few meetings hadn't panned out; neither we nor the birth moms had been taken with each other.

The birth mother, Anika, was a twenty-two-year-old East Indian lady from Fiji who was seven months pregnant.

We met her at a restaurant in her hometown, which was not too far from us.

We bought her lunch and chatted. So far, so good! She was intelligent, sweet, and gentle, and seemed ready to sign up with us.

She had looked at our life book, a book that had pictures of our life and commentary about what was important and fun for us. Apparently, it worked for her.

We left with the impression that we were all ready to move ahead.

It felt so strange that as soon as we got back from our honeymoon, we were potentially about to become parents!

It had been a nine-month wait with the adoption agency. Seems about right.

It was a wrap! We all signed papers with the agency. We were moving forward!

To make it easier to support Anika, we moved her into a house with other women. I visited her often and took her to her first doctor's appointment. She had never been to a gynecologist before, so this visit was traumatic.

In this exam and in all medical appointments after, the doctors and nurses were wonderfully supportive of her. They kept telling her what an incredible gift she was giving us.

Her pregnancy was emotionally hard for her. In her culture, it was unacceptable to be pregnant and not married.

I encouraged her to talk about all of it to try and help her release some of the emotional pain. We would go out to lunch and walk around different towns.

My friend Emma, the massage therapist, gave her a massage.

My friend Aurora had us over for dinner and we swam in her backyard pool. Anika got playful then! I was splashed unmercifully and joyfully!

Anika was tall, slender, dignified, and beautiful. In order to help the baby grow, we went shopping and she bought all the food she was used to: frozen spinach, rice, lentils, hot peppers, and such.

The doctor had prescribed folic acid and a prenatal vitamin. She devoted herself to helping this baby get what was needed.

She had grown up in Fiji in the Hindu tradition. Her family was very spiritual. She told me also that she had had no education on sex or pregnancy.

She had been extremely protected. She hadn't done anything or gone anywhere without a chaperone, that person often being her brother. She knew very little about the world.

With all her inner struggle around being unmarried and pregnant, there came a point when she said to me, "I think God meant this to happen," meaning that she was the one to give us a baby. Oh, my heart!

During this time, I was also experiencing mothering feelings. One time when I was driving to meet Anika, I was overcome with an intense feeling of claiming this baby. This child was mine! It was a very powerful, loving, protective connection in my heart—the fierce parenting instinct most mothers and fathers feel with their biological or adoptive children.

We tried to support Anika as much as we could. In July, toward the baby's due date, she came to live with us so we could be available as her contractions became regular.

One day her contractions had moved beyond Braxton-Hicks, to real contractions. I took her to the doctor, who said, "You're going to have a baby today!"

Wow! It was really happening. The hospital was five minutes from our house, which was pretty awesome.

We drove to the hospital's birthing center, where we discovered this hospital specialized in all things for children. Another amazing serendipity.

Again, all the doctors and nurses there were fantastic. They were so supportive of Anika and so encouraging. They gave her an epidural to deal with the pain.

Emma and Aurora and the adoption coordinator, Madeline, were there as added support.

Aurora knew how much this meant to us and she had brought her video camera. She videoed me in the hospital talking about how I felt while labor was happening.

Because Anika was shy around men, and even more shy about exposing her body, David wasn't allowed in the birthing room.

Anika had been going through a struggle about whether to get a look at her baby. She decided, no, she didn't want to.

The hours went on as they do. By midnight, she was fully dilated. The nurses and doctors guided her to begin pushing.

She was an absolute trouper. She followed directions as they continued to encourage her.

As the baby's head began to crown and come out, I had a few moments of panic because the head came out cone-shaped. I, the mother, forgot all my nursing. And then, something inside reminded me that this was normal. Phew!

His whole body came out. He was long and slender. The nurse gave me the scissors to cut the cord. These medical staff members were so sensitive.

He was cold, so they wrapped him in eight blankets. He came out talking, making all kinds of verbalizations that we could only surmise were him telling us about the whole journey.

Because Anika didn't want to see him, David and I were sitting in another room. The nurse brought him to us, and David was the first to hold him. Wow. Talk about an instant father. He was in love.

Later, Aurora told us that Anika had asked to see this beautiful boy she had birthed, whom we named Dylan. When Aurora brought him in to Anika, that strong birth mom looked at him and said, "Wow! I made him?! Screw my culture!" She had come to her own resolution with her pregnancy and her culture's judgment.

Pictures were taken, of course, and then the nurse put Dylan in a bassinet to wheel him to the nursery for overnight observation. The floor in the hospital had slight bumps in it so that when the wheeled cradle ran over the bumps, it jarred the bassinet. David, turning into the protective father, expressed indignation that they would let his son be bounced like that!

The nurses took care of Anika and brought her to her room for the night. We went home to our house. But who could sleep?

The next morning, I called the hospital to see how Dylan was. They said he was doing great, and we could bring him home.

Again, wow!

He was a slender baby—five pounds, fifteen ounces. Normally, six pounds is considered the magic number for a healthy baby. But they checked him over and everything worked.

Before we brought Dylan home, Anika had asked if she could see him again, so we brought him up to her room. She watched while I changed a diaper and she marveled at his tiny fingers and toes.

We are forever grateful to this brave, beautiful woman who underwent her own transformational journey and allowed us to begin one of the best transformational journeys of our lives.

Like many of you parents with your babies, I was mesmerized by my new son. The first night with him home, the second night of his life, I stayed awake gazing at him, grateful and in awe.

Most babies lose weight in their first week or two. This guy never did, thank goodness. He gained steadily. He remained long and slender and maintained a healthy weight.

I took time off from my practice to be with him. During the first week of his life, my sister and her youngest daughter came to visit. Seven-year-old Leah wanted to do everything to take care of him with me—change his diaper, feed him, and hold him.

My friend Caroline also came to visit in those early days. She thought it would be good to stay up at night with Dylan (whom we took to calling Dylly), so I could get some sleep. So sweet.

But Dylly wasn't having it. She was unable to calm him. I let her try for a while and then got up to hold him. Then we all got some sleep.

When he was two weeks old, my mother came to visit him as well.

Of course, there was a baby shower with Dylly present, and a party at our house where different folks got to hold him.

Meditation: 5-30-2021

Jesus shows up again (like yesterday). It's all about embodying Self/Light. Yesterday He said, "Follow Me." I took that to mean, "Do what I did."

Today, the word is Power—Divine Power. This is what emerges from true surrender to the Divine within. And how does one surrender? From faith and trust. From feeling safe.

We have so many levels of holding on, of keeping control, because we don't feel safe. Many of these are unconscious and have developed over this and many lifetimes on earth and elsewhere in our vast cosmos.

Originally, when we were first created by Source, we were connected at all moments to our Creator. We were safe.

Then somewhere along the line, we decided to try it alone, kind of like happens with so many milestones in human development: first steps, pushing back against parents at two years, nine years, pre-teen, teen years. And then we leave home.

Now we're on the road back home.

A Digression on Power

Power. What is it, actually? I'm learning about it.

Power is misunderstood on this planet because it's often wielded without the balancing energies of Love and Wisdom.

Those who are insecure, wounded, or lacking in self-love for whatever reason, and who seize power over others are starving for recognition and love, and crave relief from their inner emotional pain. Normally, they are out of touch with their pain but still, it exists in the unconscious, in the body, and it affects them and those around them.

No one likes pain. We want to escape it or get rid of it or heal it. But often, the path we take to dull or soothe our pain creates more pain, sometimes for others. In the case of those who seek power to relieve their inner pain, often their perspective about the effect of their actions on others is skewed.

In my EMDR (eye movement desensitization and restructuring) work with clients, this becomes clear. A person begins EMDR to relieve and heal some pain. As the work progresses and some pain is released, they often go through a process of shifting their perspective about themselves and the situation that created the pain.

Here's a quick example from my own EMDR work. Once I was working on some issue, I forget what, and after my EMDR session, I noticed that visually I saw the world differently. Colors were clearer and brighter, for instance. People I had been annoyed with looked softer, sweeter.

EMDR changes associations in the brain; areas that are too active calm down, and areas that are underactive normalize. This may lead to more of a feeling of peace.

Meditation again:

I feel El Morya (Ascended Master) come into my meditation. He works with the blue flame—the energy of Divine power, intent, will, and action. I feel the blue flame engulfing me. I notice the blue flame Angels, those wonderful beings who help facilitate absorption of the blue flame or Divine Will Light. I also noticed the Beloved I Am Presence, who is also a major helper of integration.

I also felt Archangels Michael and Faith, the male and female Archangels who work with the blue Light of Divine Power. If we trust, if we have Faith, we feel safe. We can let down our guard, our fearful need to control and let the Light within us, the Light all around us, the Light that birthed us be front and center.

Once I heard The Divine say, "Surrender to Me." I replied, "I'd love to, but how? You're going to have to help me with that too!"

Seems like I need help with everything!

I'm reminded of Jesus' instruction to, "Seek first the kingdom of God," and then everything else comes to you.

I remember another phrase, "If thine eye be single, thy whole body shall be full of light." To me, this means that if we constantly focus on Source, then things get easier.

It might seem impossible to focus on Source all the time. I've been meditating for years, and I am still a work in progress. Even if it's tough to fully achieve, though, it's worth the trying to keep getting closer.

So today the energy of Divine Will showed up. Well, it makes sense that if I'm more aligned with Divine Will, I *will* seek the Light before everything else. And then the result is that life gets easier.

And what I love so much about these inspiring nudges from Spirit is that we have so much help to accomplish our goals. There are so many wonderful Divine helpers of all kinds who appear when we ask, according to who would best serve us in each moment.

Householder Life

We were settling into our new life as parents. Dylan was thriving. I was in love.

I felt an inner nudge to start back up in my therapy practice, just a few hours a week.

We would need someone to take care of Dylan part-time. I hunted and talked to people. A woman I was acquainted with named Lily said she would be willing to be the nanny part-time, but she hadn't been around babies.

I invited my motherly, astute friend Aurora, who had been at Dylan's birth, to help me with the interview. We both agreed that Lily would do well. She was eager, sincere, kind, and gentle. I hired her and went back to work part-time.

That felt good. I was a mom first, and I was also a therapist. In work, I was filling another need. Lily stayed with us for a few months. My practice was picking up again and I needed another caregiver who could devote more time to Dylan.

I always took Dylly for walks to our local park in his stroller. I got my exercise and he got to see more of the world.

One day when we were in the kid's play section of the park, I noticed a young woman with a little girl close in age to Dylan.

I watched her for a while and liked how she interacted with her little one.

It also kind of looked like she wasn't the mother of this child. She was young.

I talked to her and found out her name was Hannah, and that she was a daycare provider for Lisa, who was a year older than Dylan. She was providing daycare in Lisa's home nearby.

As we talked, I found myself liking her and told her I was looking for a daycare person for Dylan. We agreed to meet at Lisa's home to explore more of this possible relationship.

At our interview, I learned that Hannah had daycare training and credentials and was signed up on a local registry. She was the real thing.

We decided to go ahead part-time at Lisa's home. Lisa's mom was good with the arrangement.

This relationship with Hannah lasted for about two and a half years until Dylly was ready for preschool at age three. At one point, she took on more children and moved into her own space. Then it really looked like a daycare. Hannah loved the children and provided appropriate toys, nap times, and such.

During these years I was still at St. Francis Church, singing in the choir, going to Taizé prayer, and doing contemplative meditation with my friend, Katherine, on Saturdays.

I was also beginning to feel a limit with the Catholic teachings. My perspective was changing, partly because of my psychotherapy education, but also reflective of my own psychological and spiritual growth.

It felt to me that, whereas some of the rules seemed designed to help folks lead a good life, it also seemed that they could keep people at a childlike development.

Obeying rules created by the Church was supposed to make you a good Catholic. But these were imposed by Church hierarchy, though some would say they came from God.

What about questioning those mandates to come to your own relationship with the Divine? What if you didn't need the intermediary of a priest to connect you to God by giving you Communion? What if you could go directly to Source; just you and Creator?

It reminded me of phases of human growth. As teenagers, we normally push back against our parents. We question them.

As teens, we are in a process of differentiating, determining how we are separate from who our parents are and what they have taught us. This is healthy, normal, and necessary for us to become fully integrated, individualized grownups.

I valued so much of what was present in the Catholic tradition, the wonderful mystics I had read who had discovered their own relationship with the Divine, the music, and the rituals designed to enhance connection to Spirit.

I also saw people in church going through the motions because they felt they had to: showing up *en masse* (ha!) for Christmas or Easter, but not living or pursuing a deeper understanding or connection of themselves with their expanded Self.

This definitely doesn't apply to all Catholics, but many of the folks I was in contact with were not so interested in going deep.

It is interesting that I also never felt Jesus very strongly while I was involved in the Catholic experience. I tried, I asked, but that connection didn't materialize until I later pursued other spiritual avenues.

It had been Jesus who got me started on this spiritual road back in Cambridge, Massachusetts, when I was having lunch in my backyard. That powerful occurrence was a major motivation for me to pursue spiritual concerns and ultimately led me into the Catholic Church.

I was feeling that the church helped support me during a stage in my spiritual sojourn, but also that I had grown out of it. Maybe I was becoming a spiritual teenager!

Meditation: 5-31-2021

Lanto (Ascended Master) helping me absorb the Gold Flame (flame of wisdom, Christ mind). Then I feel the seven basic flames—rose pink, blue, indigo, emerald-green, violet, crystalline, and gold—dancing in, through, and around me. I understand that in our evolution we absorb, integrate, and manifest all seven.

Rose pink is for Divine Love; blue is for Divine Power; indigo is for Divine passion and devotion; emerald green is for healing, balance, and love; violet is for purifying, ritual, and alchemy; gold is for Divine Wisdom; crystalline is for embodying all the flames—Source energy.

I hear the words of Sai Baba – "Man minus ego equals God".

I talk to my ego and love it and bring in the Hawaiian Ho'oponopono prayer:

"I'm sorry, please forgive, thank you, I love you."

I notice the three-fold flame activating in my heart—the pink, yellow, and blue flames of love, wisdom, and power. We all have this invisible spiritual flame in our hearts.

Try tuning into (imagine) the pink, yellow, and blue flames (usually small at first, and often of unequal size) in the middle of your chest. When you get a sense or picture of your flames, see their size equalizing. Sit with this and just see what happens.

When you notice that they seem to be the same size, imagine them all growing bigger until, if you want, you see them larger than your body. You are immersed in them. Hang out with them for a bit. Notice how you feel.

Working with this flame helps to balance the love, wisdom, and power elements within us, facilitating integration of our Divine Self.

The flame becomes big, engulfing all of me. I soak in its energy.

I hear, "Source Generator, and Source Code."

I have heard "Source Code" other times in meditation. I will wait to see what that is.

I feel how we can recharge ourselves as we take time to meditate, to connect with Source. Just like our cell phone batteries need daily recharging, we do too. Without our connection to Source, we stumble.

All comes from Source. We eat the fresh food enervated by our Sun, which receives its energy stepped down in charge from Source through the Great Central Sun of our galaxy, and we are renewed.

We sleep to recharge. We exercise.

We relax in nature, feeling a direct link to Source. So many of us feel the Creator through nature—our church—and we are renewed.

Source is Always
Sending Support

A week ago, as I write this, I had an energetic clearing from a long-time friend I met at a spiritual conference. She has expanded exponentially into her True Self and does wonderful work bringing Love frequency into Earth and helping to remove the distortions around Source.

This week, I have felt very different. I had doubts about myself, so I felt I needed some ego clearing. I wondered if all the spiritual work I have been doing was off. I emailed my friend, and she reassured me that for two weeks there would be a lot of shifting and weirdness. Not to worry. After a few days, I felt clearer and had more energy.

I talked to another friend, and she was also supportive and referred me to another spiritual transmitter in the UK, Jacqueline. I've been vibing off her offerings and listening, watching, and absorbing what she is creating. This is truly a wonderful, unique gift from Source.

Dylan's Growth

Parenting Dylan was a joy. He was a beautiful child. (That wasn't just my biased view as a mother; others told me too!)

He was quite outgoing. I would wheel him in the stroller down the block. We would see a group of swaggery teenage boys. He would wave and say, "Hey, guys!"

They were a bit surprised to hear this little kid shout out to them. And they all responded, "Hey, how ya doin'?"

Dylan began his crawling and walking adventure by crawling backward. Oftentimes we needed to rescue him from under a coffee table or chair that he had successfully lodged himself under.

Of course, like many kids, standing upright and beginning to walk was accompanied by occasional head bumps and some panic from his parents.

He was learning to talk, not always understanding the significance of what he was saying, and sometimes drawing attention to us in comical ways.

Once when I was in the credit union depositing checks, I was holding him at the teller's window. He loudly popped out with, "Mom, are you naked?" You can imagine that we suddenly became the focus of everyone within hearing distance!

I also liked to play with situations that came up in public places. One day, I was in the check-out line at our local co-op with Dylan seated in the shopping cart in the backward-facing seat.

A guy behind us also in the line piped up with, "He's staring at me a lot; do I look like his father?" I responded, "I have no idea what his father looks like." Dead silence after that!

I really *didn't* know what Dylan's birth father looked like. We had never met him. Due to legal procedures, and with the help of our adoption attorney, we went through the requisite steps to try to reach him to let him know he had a son.

He had a right to be part of the process. I'm sure he would have no idea that we were posting a notice in the local paper addressed to him. He would have had no clue about adoption laws in the U.S. or even to look in a newspaper to check.

When I took Dylly out in the stroller or to the grocery store, we often would be approached by people who thought I was his nanny. I was white with white hair. He was a little brown boy. Folks couldn't put it together that I was his mom.

Dylan and I got used to this. As he grew older, in response to people's queries, he would say, "That's my mom. I'm adopted."

When Dylly was three years old, our family went to China to visit David's aunt Alison and her husband Sam, who were living in Shenzhen province at the southmost tip of mainland China. It was a remarkable trip.

Those who have traveled halfway around the world know the crazy long ten-hour plane ride. Mom and Dad, unable to sleep, provided the double-lap bed for Dylan, who had no problem sleeping and was refreshed when we landed in Taipei, the first leg of our trip. There, we were greeted with a giant sign in the airport, "Drug Trafficking Punishable by Death!" Well, that was welcoming.

We caught our next flight to Hong Kong. There, we were met by Sam, who shepherded us the rest of the way. We boarded the Star ferry for Shenzhen province, the town of Shekou, where Sam and Alison lived in ex-pat housing. Sam was employed by an oil company that was working with China.

On the ferry, we filled out forms explaining why we were traveling to China, how long we planned to stay, and such. Sam said we needed to be exact and accurate, which was a bit intimidating.

Even more intimidating, offboarding the ferry in Shekou, we were ushered into a building where Chinese police, holding semi-automatic weapons, kept guard making sure no one caused any trouble. That was quite another welcome!

We waited there for a long while until it was our turn and—miracle of miracles—they let us into the country.

It had been an exhausting twenty-four-hour trip.

At Alison and Sam's very large, beautiful ex-pat house, we wanted to sleep but were encouraged to try and stay awake until local bedtime. Then we could acclimatize to the rhythm of this part of the world more quickly. For the moment, this meant more exhaustion.

Alison was so glad to have us there! And she was the consummate hostess and tour guide.

She took us to local markets where she bought delicious falling-off-the-bone mutton from the Muslim shops.

We "ran the gauntlet," as she put it, fending off folks who positioned themselves strategically on this very wide sidewalk leading to a large marketplace, trying to sell us, the white, rich Americans, their one item.

Their tactic was to come very close to us and talk, talk, talk in Cantonese or Mandarin, with forceful insistence, while shoving their wares in our faces. "No" from us was not in their vocabulary.

A tactic that Alison showed us was to acknowledge and just keep walking, without engaging. It was great practice for us to set boundaries mainly within ourselves.

Alison had learned Mandarin and she knew the local customs, so she was a master negotiator when it was required.

We ate noodles at a well-known noodle joint. When we got the bill, Alison saw that we were being gouged because we were foreigners. She proceeded to argue fiercely with the manager, who wasn't backing down. Eventually, Alison threw down the money she knew was fair, and we left.

One day, we attended a cultural festival where different ethnic groups performed their unique dances. We learned that at that time there were seventy-two different ethnic groups in China.

That night, we were entertained by a light and sound extravaganza, with dancers waving long, colorful ribbons.

One weekend, we got on a plane to Xi'an where the terracotta warriors and their horses stand guard in a large warehouse. You walked around the narrow pathway on the perimeter of the building looking at the display. You weren't supposed to take pictures, but I did. I didn't get caught either!

Meditation: 6-8-2021

Asking to connect with Source, my personal connection to Source. I am aware of some anger surfacing. I notice it. It feels like a connection to my mother. I remember her anger that was mostly underground, not expressed.

And an incident reported when she was in therapy. The therapist was asking her to do some work. She got mad and fired the therapist. I notice further that my anger seems to also relate to styles of change in me that feel abrupt or forced.

Giving it time, I notice clear, refined gold light permeating my bodies. I hear "Immerse yourself in Source. Source immersion. Let Source unlock your unique Source codes to facilitate easier release of non-Source." My body relaxes further.

I hear the question, "What color is love?" In this space, I feel crystal clear gold with a tinge of pink.

I feel joy in the form of laughter bubbling up. Whole body laughter, every cell and muscle and bone laughing uproariously in love. Laughter as medicine. Laughter as the way.

Immerse yourself in Source.

In China, we saw a monument to Yang Guifei and visited the Forest of Steles. (For more information see travelchinaguide.com)

Alison had a Chinese friend whose daughter was about five years old. This friend had tried and tried to get pregnant and had finally succeeded. Because China was limiting children to one per family at that time, this mom was super protective of her little girl. Dylan got to play with her, and we went to kids' playgrounds and small amusement parks, and ponds to feed koi.

Eating out was an adventure. At a restaurant, we would be seated with a number of other people around a large, round table with a Lazy Susan in the middle. The waiters would bring the dishes and put them on the spinning center disc, allowing everyone to partake. Including beer, our tab for four people came to $25.

Alison had a teacher friend who had set up an English class for her fellow teachers with Alison as the teacher. One evening, we all went to Alison's English class and at the conclusion, the Chinese teachers got to practice their English with us. That was fun. They were learning a lot.

Folks in China loved Dylan. He was a cute, young, brown boy. They all wanted to take their picture with him.

One day, one Chinese woman saw Dylan and, before any of us could act, she grabbed him by the hand to pose with her family. Of course, Dyl was scared and ran back to us.

The woman came over, looked at me with my white skin and white hair, and looked puzzled. I mimed that I was the mom. She clearly didn't believe me. Lots of puzzlement there. No picture for her that day. She scared the boy.

Alison had a good-sized library in her house, including several books that were banned in China. These books recorded history that the government didn't want citizens to know about. I read some of them when I was there and ordered some when I got back to the states.

One that was particularly upsetting was *The Rape of Nanking*. It talks about mass murder and mass rape by the Japanese against the people of Nanking, the capital of China at that time during the Second Sino-Japanese War (1937-1945).

One day Sam took us on a tour of a village in the countryside. There were rows and rows of carefully maintained crops laid out on a mountain, watered by villagers carrying buckets of water suspended one on each end of a pole that they carried on their shoulders.

These were extremely poor people. The bathroom was the railroad tracks above their two-room huts. The huts had tin roofs and three sides to each room. Where the fourth wall would have been, we could see into their meager furnishings. But they each had a TV, electricity, and a mailbox. One room was for the family, the second was for the pigs.

Because these folks lived on a mountain, we had been climbing to get there. I was not in shape for that. And we still had climbing to do to get to a view! I think I put a halt to the uppermost height! I gained great admiration for all their strong muscles.

When we were descending and going back past the huts, it was dinnertime. We were invited by one family to join them. Sam graciously refused but took pictures of us with the family. They were pleased and all smiles. Owning so little, they were rich in heart and generosity.

I didn't learn Mandarin or Cantonese or Taishanese or any of the seventy-two other dialects when I was there. But I did learn to say "hello" ("ni hao") and "thank you" ("xié xié"). I did a lot of "ni hao" to the ever-present police, who just looked at me; though some nodded.

I grew an appreciation for the endless stream of bicycles on the roads. And I became very grateful for traffic laws in the U.S.

If, in being driven somewhere, we arrived at a three-, four-, or five-way intersection, the rules were that you just went for it, avoiding collisions as you could. I'm sure I created deep Ann-shaped handprints in my armrests.

For our two weeks there, I also had a chronic sore throat from the pollution. I believe these days there are attempts to curtail that problem.

We were also impressed by the bigness of the Chinese style. Everywhere were huge apartment buildings reaching to the sky, much larger than any I had seen in the U.S., built to house the vast population. Washing hung off balconies, and they were all different pastel colors: pink, green, blue, and yellow. And the ever-present humongous cranes loomed, swinging in space to build more.

Now and then, we would hear loud booms. Alison told us they were demolishing mountains and dumping the soil into the Shenzhen Bay to create more land. Nothing was too big to tackle!

Because Shekou was an Economic Free Trade Zone, it was supposed to offer more job opportunities for the population. If you were not a local resident, you needed a visa to enter. Many people tried to enter the area. Jobs must have been hard to come by in general.

Visiting China for a short time gave me a view of this culture I never would have had otherwise. I developed an idea that I would like to live in different places around the world and get to know the personalities of local folks—how they thought and felt, and what was important to them. I thought I wanted to write these observations all down in a book. At the time, this was a very strong impulse.

I did not live in different locales and write about the people, but perhaps my wish was granted in another way.

In my therapy practice, I have sat with folks of many cultures from all over the world and I have gotten to know each one more deeply than I most likely would have if I had merely been living in proximity to them.

I am privileged and grateful that folks trust me enough to open up to me about their deepest fears, wishes, habits, and likes, and that they are willing to have a relationship with me so that together we can uncover who they really are and help them meet their life goals.

As I write, I am struck that this is a lot like midwifery. When I was ready to move on from being an RN, I researched midwifery and toyed with the idea of becoming a midwife.

On our last day with Alison and Sam, we went to Hong Kong to trip around before our flight. We rode the Peak Tram, a cable-pulled car that carries people from Central Hong Kong up a very steep hill to the top of Victoria Peak. It has been operating since 1988.

Alison didn't want us to leave. At lunch, she kept the conversation going so long that we almost missed our flight!

When we got to the airport, David put Dylan on his shoulders, and we ran to our gate. Phew! We made it in time, but barely.

I seem to have blocked out the adventures of the return trip, but I have very good memories of China Air. Returning to the U.S., we flew on a double-decker jet. Both coming and going, the flight attendants took very good care of us. They had great food and great service.

What I do remember from traveling west to east and back again, is that I checked up often on the up-to-date flight progress screen at the front of the cabin. On the long flight, I was like that kid on a long car ride: "Are we there yet?!" I don't sleep on planes and I'm not crazy about sitting still for long periods. Must be my fiery Aries nature!

50

Spirit Provides

It was time for Dylly to go to preschool. I scoped out several schools, mainly Waldorf and Montessori. That fit with my sense of how to raise kids. I settled on one that wasn't too far from our house, a Montessori. I really liked the two women who ran it and felt good with the staff, their philosophy, and what they offered.

For Dyl to go to preschool, he needed to be potty trained. School started in the fall, so we had the summer to see if that would happen.

It turned out that Dylan was ready. Potty training was a breeze. No stress there.

Like a lot of kids on their first day of school, Dylan was not happy that I was leaving him in a strange place with people who were unfamiliar to him.

One of the staff picked him up, held him, and motioned for me to just go, as my son cried and looked at me with sad eyes. My heart broke, but I went. I had some comfort in knowing that this sweet young lady was holding and talking to him. I hoped he would be okay.

Later, they told me he was just fine after he couldn't see me. They had dance, story time, blocks, coloring, and all manner of fun things for these young humans.

Dylly flourished in this Montessori space. I was told that at dance time, he was the first one out there rocking and jiving to the music. He had some moves apparently!

The staff was wonderful. I loved their caring, their firm yet gentle boundary-making, and their understanding of what makes three-to-five-year-old kids tick. The head teacher became an occasional babysitter for Dylan.

The time came for kindergarten, which meant more decisions.

I searched out schools: first our neighborhood school. I knew one of the parents, who was a grandparent raising his granddaughter. She had been removed from her mom's care due to her mom's drug use. This little girl sometimes acted out because of her emotional trauma. She responded well to kindness, patience, and understanding.

I sat in on the kindergarten class that this young child was in. At one point the teacher yelled at her, chastising her—for what, I could not decipher. The girl was not acting out at that moment.

Ok, that school was out.

I visited another school that had a good reputation and philosophy, especially about diversity. It was okay, but I didn't feel especially jazzed about it.

I looked up Montessori elementary schools, but there didn't seem to be any that were public. I seem to remember there was a private one, but it was too expensive for us. It was also just forming. I ruled that one out.

I decided to talk with the two women who ran the Montessori school we were in. I trusted them and they knew Dylan.

They talked to me about Waldorf methods and suggested that Dylan's style might fit in very well with that approach. It works with the whole child, right and left sides of the brain, creative and cognitive.

It uses movement to promote brain development. Art and music are part and parcel of the curriculum, employed in such a way as to support the more cognitive subjects like math, science, history, and literature.

The kids learn crafts, like finger knitting, that support the development of fine and gross motor movement. Nature walks occur regularly. From first grade on, the kids memorize poems and participate in plays that they perform for parents and the class. And there was much more.

There were Waldorf schools around that were private and too expensive for us. There was also a well-established public one that was within doable driving distance and part of the city school district.

I visited their kindergarten class and knew right away. This was the one!

The teacher sang with the kids and often even sang her directions. The kids got to move a lot, sit on the floor, do puzzles, dance, paint, listen at story time, and do more activities that seemed to me perfect for this age.

The only stumbling block was that there was a lottery to get in.

David agreed with me about the school, and I filled out the forms. We got the results, and we were on the waiting list, something like third from the top. Eek. Only if some people backed out would we get in.

I really wanted this to be the school. I did my version of prayer with great gusto and heart.

We waited. And due to some miracle of Source, we got in!

This school was K–8, so we were set for some years. I was ecstatic.

In Waldorf, in either first or third grade, the kids start with a new teacher, who will be with them all the way through eighth grade. Our teacher from first grade was a man who was a musician and artist who, as we discovered, grew to love these kids deeply. He was involved.

In Waldorf, the understanding of child development is that most kids live in an imaginative world until about nine years of age. At that time, their brains have matured to the point that they begin to access their cognitive skills.

The overall Waldorf idea involves supporting the normal growth of a child physically, mentally, and emotionally, so they can become the whole, unique person they are meant to be.

As a result of this observation, reading is not taught until third grade. Up until that point, a lot of prep work goes on to maximize the success of this next stage of growth.

Particular types of movement, handwork, fine motor skills, and drawing of particular shapes are taught, all meant to prepare the body and mind for reading and writing.

I liked this style. It was found to be counterproductive to push a child into a stage of development that they weren't ready for biologically, emotionally, or mentally.

Let the child develop normally. Support and enhance their growth so that each successive stage builds upon the firm foundation of the fully ripened previous stages (much like Abraham Maslow's Hierarchy of Needs chart for emotional growth). That way, the child successfully realizes each phase with ease and grace.

And so, years of being a school parent began.

During these next sixteen years, which included his graduating from college, my primary occupation was parenting Dylan.

I simultaneously ran my private practice and looked at ways I could enhance it, explored my spiritual life, researched ways to maximize my health, and, of course, did all the family events that a person does.

During this time, I was also questioning my marital relationship. That seemed to be the one aspect of my life that was not growing. I took us to marriage counseling and prayed and meditated about it. Things weren't changing. In my meditation, I kept feeling that it was important to hang in there until Dylan was done with high school. So, I did.

A relationship is between two people, so I know I had a part in it.

When the time came to separate, we were both in agreement that that was the best course. We found a lawyer who guided us through the lengthy legal process: how to fill out all the forms, file them with the court, and serve each other. We were doing this ourselves.

We had decided to do a legal separation so I could stay on David's health insurance. We found our own separate lawyers who looked over the legal separation settlement agreement. We made a few changes and that was that.

It was a very friendly, equitable agreement.

51

Spirit Meets You Where You Are

Meanwhile, back in the spiritual department...
Always looking to deepen my connection to Spirit, during these years I explored more spiritual styles. I read Joshua David Stone's books. He had been a psychotherapist turned spiritual teacher.

He wrote many books about what he discovered in his journey. His work spoke to me. I tried out some of his meditations and prayers and felt powerful Divine energy from them. For years, I have adopted some of his approaches when I am leading meditations.

Like with all skill development, I found that repeated use of these methods (besides my own therapy work) helped release what was preventing me from accessing my own Light to increase its shining within.

From his writings, I also learned about and encountered beautiful, heart-filled beings on other planes of creation who, with an invitation from me, also helped me release mental and emotional blocks and prompt activation of my own Light. I talk with and am grateful to these Source-connected forms of Light today.

One of my friends, a mom of a classmate of Dylan's, was also exploring her spirituality. We got to know each other, and she invited me to check out a guy who was offering a spiritual conference in Las Vegas. I did. He looked interesting, so the two of us decided to attend.

This conference was two or three days. The energy there was good, strong, and expansive. We met other people on their spiritual paths. It felt like a place to grow.

For a few more years, we attended his workshops—held in Flagstaff, Roswell, Cambria, and Las Vegas again—and made good friendships with other folks there.

I am grateful for these times of more clearing, expanding spiritually, and learning.

After a time, I felt that I was ready to move on. It was time for me to begin holding my own classes.

During these years, I also was experimenting in my therapy practice. Some clients were pursuing their spiritual growth. Together we decided to try out a few of the spiritual clearing and energizing tools I had learned to help them release their emotional and mental blocks.

They loved it. I loved it. I felt energized each time I would guide them through a process. They gave me feedback that they felt calmer, lighter, clearer, and more joyful.

This was to become a favorite style of mine. I created a website that talked about it and added the phrase "exploration of spirituality" to my *Psychology Today* site.

Many of my clients found me on the *Psychology Today* site because spirituality was exactly what they wanted to dive into to help them grow.

I began to experiment with holding spiritual classes. I created and guided many workshops on varying subjects from chakra clearing to the seven basic Light Rays of Source and more.

Sometimes a friend and I would join up and lead these events together.

One of my favorites was teaming up with Judy to create a play shop for six to ten-year-olds.

We said, "No parents allowed!"

The kids entered the magical play shop world we had created by receiving a crown woven of flowers. We provided pictures of nature elementals fairies, elves, chakras, etc.—that they could color.

We showed them how to use a pendulum to help a person feel better. We had a treasure hunt with clues that resulted in them getting a prize of a sparkly bag containing a crystal and other small, magical items.

I read a story to them I had downloaded from a meditation called "The Rabbit Who Jumped So High"—complete with pictures!

My son and his friend also came to help us guide the kids. Afterward, he said he felt very comfortable there. He's good with kids.

The kids told their parents how much fun they had, and the parents wanted a play shop all for themselves!

Meditation intermission!

Meditation: 6-23-2021

Connecting to Source

Remembering years ago, when I felt a strong wave of love energy in meditation and heard from Source, "You are mine." I had felt claimed in a way I had never felt before in this life, that I belonged to someone very powerfully. It was a source of inspiration for me to pursue that relationship even more.

And today, I remember that quote of "seek ye first the kingdom of God." Or "let thine eye be single"—meaning focus constantly on the Divine.

And today, I am feeling that Love is inviting Love—me—into deeper connection, that together, we are unbeatable.

I feel my growing receptivity to love in my mind, my heart, and all my physical cells. I feel that a key is to tap into my own particular Source code. Each one of us has our own code, our own way.

And it feels like part of the key is to release the need to control the outcome, to surrender to Love in trust, knowing that Love has our back.

As Love enters the cells of our heart, mind, and body, as we participate and agree to our own transformation with ease and grace, Light enters us and changes us physically, mentally, and emotionally.

Because we have free will, this happens with our agreeing to it.

And more Light is born; we are the garden and the fruit. We have prepared our soil, all parts of us, to receive Light. We want it. We trust it. We have been seeking the greatest adventure of all—to be Light in the flesh.

And I am reminded that this is a joyful phenomenon. I have encountered the humor and playfulness of the Divine themselves.

In meditation, I have run and skipped with the Divine while we become like two young children.

I have heard Source saying that they can be whatever we need at the time.

If we need them to be a parent, we can burrow snugly into their deep, warm, loving lap.

If we need them to be a peer, we can have a one-to-one conversation with them.

And likewise, each time I come upon an Ascended Being of some sort, I may feel their goofiness or lighthearted nature.

Each one of us who moves on to another plane of existence retains our own personality.

Correspondingly, those individuals from wherever who dwell in areas unseen to our eyes and who are of the Light have their own unique nature.

I have worked with a doctor from Sirius who is definitely not serious in nature. To me he's like a little elf who dances lightly all around. He is very focused, very respectful, very devoted to his healing work, and very powerful in his Light.

Saint Germain, Ascended Being, can be very funny and playful, a regular jokester in his intentional messages of Love.

Meditation: 6-25-2021

Connecting to Source. About an hour. Letting go more and more of the subtleties of my control, fear, ego.

Relaxing, trusting, based on a new, all-encompassing experience of Light, Love.

Releasing the other experiences of perceived and real danger through so many lifetimes, events that reverberate in my physical, mental, emotional, and astral bodies. Memories that are being subsumed in the all-loving Light that creates existence.

I sit. And am encouraged to go beyond what I am familiar with, to trust more deeply.

I feel the chakras of the fifth dimension, crystal clear light with lavender, varieties of crystalline-white, pink-gold, magenta, violet-gold, blue-gold, and platinum.

I hear, "This is a jumping-off point to go the limit. To go all the way."

However many "dimensions" or perspectives there are of Light—some have said ninety-six; some say three hundred fifty-two—I hear, "It doesn't matter." What matters is your relationship and complete surrender to Light as it is created for your particular Source code.

I feel rose pink enter me. Love. I hear, "To be fully Love in all cells of all bodies." I feel Mother Mary, Kuthumi, Amora, Orion—different manifestations of Love, each with their own signature purpose, like us.

We are all alike in that way; we are all equal in Light. Light creates Love. Let Light lead.

I feel the Mahatma, Avatar of Synthesis, at the three hundred fifty second level of creation, a community of Light consciousness that helps us integrate Light. I am reconnecting with familiar faces. That in itself helps me relax.

I have been meditating with Oracle Girl, Jacqueline, from the UK. She is blowing it all out of the water. I am loving what she offers and how. I am growing into my Self more. She invites us to release all attachments to all identities, spiritual and otherwise, to be our Self.

I question all the connections I have made spiritually. I hear her say, "Never doubt yourself. All leads to All."

I am clearing my space. Lots of Goodwill donations. Purging. Boxes of paper to shred. It feels easy and lightening. I go through papers from Dylan's early years (he is twenty-four years old now) and my heart expands. He likes some of his preschool art too!

I share pictures from successive events in Dylan's life with someone else, from birth on. My heart is filled with love.

I am ok with not knowing where this is going. My meditations have shifted; the ones I lead and my personal silent time. I feel the reality of what Jacqueline is talking about—nature, the Earth, us, the universe.

I am not sure of where this is taking me in terms of work or otherwise. I am letting go and enjoying the ride!

Coming Home

Where are you in your journey right now? When you drop your awareness down into your body, what do you feel?

The journey to Light reveals through the body, grounding your experience of Oneness in your own particular way.

Do you feel Peace? Joy? Love? Freedom? Gratitude?

Are you tense somewhere in your neck, shoulders, or abdomen?

Your body loves you dearly and communicates how it's really going down for you in the moment. In relationship with your body, you learn how you really feel.

Can you stay with this information? There is no judgment from the body, just information.

Many of us learn to disconnect from our bodies, especially when we have been hurt. Hurt lives in the body.

We don't want pain, so we find ways to avoid it. We live in our heads, for instance, and ignore the body. That is until the body yells so loudly that we can't avoid it any longer, through pain or illness.

Our body reminds us that in the experience of being on this planet, we are in bodies. We feel, see, touch, hear, smell, taste, and feel pain.

We have a mind. We think.

We have a heart. We have emotions.

Light, Pure Love, the Source of Love, also invites us to be in the space of infinite possibilities and probabilities, at the quantum level. Here all is created. Here you can be in those luscious experiences of joy, love, and freedom.

And you get to be the joy, the gratitude, the possibilities; all of this in your body.

Love is a Relationship with Yourself and Source

When you love someone dearly and you make love, you share a deep intimacy, a deep communication physically, mentally, emotionally, and spiritually with this other person.

You are in relationship, first, with all parts of you. You love yourself, all parts of you. Then you are in relationship with another. Being and staying connected to you and loving you, you are more available to the other and for the experience together.

The same is true for your own special connection with Source and all that entails.

As with another, you gradually get to know Source. Trust is built.

As you begin to trust that Other, you relax and allow yourself to receive.

Pure Love also gives you opportunities to release old patterns—mental, physical, emotional—that keep you from experiencing all there is to experience.

Perhaps you find yourself in a situation where your heart opens wide, and you feel profound love. Or you experience loss, and your heart breaks open in grief.

These feelings are in the body.

Can you stay with them? Can you flow with the energy of deep emotion?

These feelings take you deeper into the domain of Pure Love.

Source, Pure Love, keeps inviting you into relationship with yourself and with the Light of Themself. Source pursues you as you, in accord with your nature.

Then, as you trust the process and begin to feel that Love is leading you, you can let go of your former patterns of protection.

You can open to the support, intelligence, harmony, balance, and love of the community of all of creation, nature, and positive inter-dimensional Light beings, in the way that is best for you and in harmony with your makeup.

You realize you are never alone. You begin to experience a peace that pervades your whole body, mind, feelings, and spirit.

You realize you are home, and all is well.

That feeling can be true wherever you are, whomever you're with, whatever is happening.

Not that upsets won't arise. But you have an anchor in Love through one or more of the many connections in your spiritual support system.

Using your spiritual tools, you can reset back to ground, which is you as Pure Love.

And throughout your life, Source is always there, relentlessly pursuing you, available, and waiting. Source invites you to open up to the Love that you are.

Since we are all connected in this vast creation, as you embody more of the Love that you are, you activate your own creative gifts. By expressing them, you enhance Everyone and Everything.

This is Your Trip Home

I invite you to continue this journey or begin this adventure in your own manner. Wherever you are in relationship to Source or even to just the idea that there might be something besides Earth-based evolution, consider it a playful voyage. Be like a child discovering the world for the first time.

My dad encouraged me to write my story. I have done this.

He knew I was interested in spirituality, though he and my mom weren't. I would go visit him and my mom in New Jersey and talk about some of my experiences with Sant Keshavadas, or the Catholic Church.

When I was thinking of becoming a nun, my parents took me out of their will because they didn't want me giving their money to the Catholic Church. I can honor their point of view. They didn't like a lot about the Church, especially how women were viewed.

I think I got back in their good graces when I didn't enter the convent!

I'm still not sure why my dad encouraged me. He was the writer in the family. He wrote books, he wrote for work, and he wrote articles for journals.

He and my mom loved words. They had the whole twenty-volume set of the *New English Oxford Dictionary,* published in 1989. They talked about interesting words and their origins.

My mom filled in crossword puzzles for years, the *New York Times* daily and Sunday crosswords. We bought her books of crosswords. She spent hours on them. Words and writing were always in our milieu.

I'm grateful for my dad's support. I feel it still. And perhaps I've inherited some of his ability to write, or at least the motivation.

I wonder about the power of words. The energy in a word. Either spoken or read or sung.

This reminds me of words in the Bible: "In the beginning was the Word." (John 1:1) What does that mean?

Does that mean Sound or an actual spoken or sung Word as a creative force, or both? A force that has to do with birthing. In this case, maybe birthing all of creation.

Music or speech affects our minds, emotions, bodies, and spirits. Sound affects each of us differently. Words convey pictures, ideas, and experiences.

The written word often seems inadequate to transmit the whole of an occurrence. The sound portion isn't there.

That's why I've included the meditation suggestions here, to give you a guide into a different way of perceiving. If you tried out some of them, what did you feel?

If you're interested in participating in our Zoom meditations, my friend Anna and I have uploaded some of our Saturday morning meditations onto YouTube. They are on my channel, Ann Naimark. They're each about twenty minutes long.

We've been offering these freely for about two years to aid folks in re-centering after their work week and especially during this time in the world. If you want to participate live, send me your email via my website: www.annnaimark.com. It would be lovely to see you either way!

I've found, as have friends and clients, that as you luxuriate in a meditation, your mind quiets, your emotions relax, and you encounter something else—something that may bring you to a different way of being, of living. People often comment that they feel calm, deeply at peace, energized, and happy.

My hope is also that in reading this opus, the words will not only convey pictures and ideas, to your mind, but give you a felt sense of what touched me in my exploits, and that that visceral impression will help open up areas, questions, in your life that will lead you to curiosity. To "What if?"

"What if I check out this idea that's been floating around in my brain? What if I pay attention to this feeling that doesn't go away about doing this thing that I've never done before?"

And that those explorations lead you to vistas that satisfy your need for joy, peace, and adventure.

I hope that the words printed here coming from my meditations also give you a heartfelt sense of the Other, that is us, that is Love. And that that touch activates in you a desire to also seek, in your way, a relationship with Source, with Love, that opens you to those infinite possibilities and probabilities in your life.

My heart's desire is that you find your Self, living life your way, in peace, harmony, joy, love, and freedom. And in finding your Self, you also find the vastness of community in Light, both on the earth and, perhaps, in other realms. That in finding your "people" you receive the support you need to continue with your quest.

And then you know you are home.

Acknowledgments

So many people to thank!

Christine Kloser and crew (including Carrie Jareed, my book concierge) for guiding me through every step of this writing and publishing process. I never realized it was so much work!! Thank you all for your patience.

Ron San Miguel ("Modern Day Mystic") who became a partner in book-writing crime—AIC (Ass In Chair to get it done!)—who got his book done first and who has helped guide and support me in my process. You're a great friend.

My friends who read the raw manuscript and offered helpful feedback: Anna Kato, Sandra Warne, Desiree Aragon, and Karen Takayama.

My blog coach, Dr. Karen Finn, who taught me so much about blog writing. We had so much fun in our Zoom calls. I miss you!

All my teachers in every way over the years. You know who you are. You have added to my life in ways I can't even begin to fathom from elementary school through junior high, high school, college, graduate school, nursing school, and workshops, from loving chemistry in high school to psychology in college to group therapy in grad school. My piano teacher, Capitola Dickerson, from third to twelfth grade, you enhanced my love of music enormously.

My multiple choir teachers: elementary, college, and church.

All my spiritual teachers and there were many over the years, who each had a part in my journey of the spirit.

All my friends who taught me important things about relationship.

My love relationships, who also helped me grow in the area of intimacy.

My beautiful son Dylan, who has taught me so much about being a mom and a friend, about boundaries, and about critical thinking—slowing down and considering before I jump to a conclusion, who teaches me about technology and coaches me in making YouTube videos, website ideas, and more, who has added untold joy to my life and allowed me to experience love that grows and matures as he has grown and matured. What a blessing to have you in my life!

Spiritual Quotations

Here are 101 spiritual quotations to support you when you're feeling overwhelmed.

And also uplift, reassure, calm, and make you laugh!

Some are from my meditation, and some are from folks you've no doubt heard of. And because I love Rumi so much, I've included a bunch of his quotes. Take and enjoy!

1. When I find myself in times of trouble, Mother Mary comes to me, speaking words of wisdom, "Let it be." —Paul McCartney

2. Don't give up now. Chances are your best kiss, your hardest laugh, and your greatest day are still yet to come. —Atticus

3. Nothing is impossible. The word itself says, "I'm Possible." —Audrey Hepburn (Attributed)

4. You've always had the power, my dear. You just had to learn it for yourself. —Glinda, *The Wizard of Oz* (film)

5. A true hero isn't measured by the size of his strength, but by the strength of his heart. —Zeus, Disney's *Hercules*

6. I Am That I Am. —Divine (Exodus 3:14)

7. I Am the Resurrection and the Life. I Am the Embodiment of the Light. —Jesus (From meditation)

8. I Am the Soul, I Am the Love Divine, I Am Light, I Am Will, I Am God's Design. —Djwahl Kuhl, Ascended Master (Attributed)

9. Your work is to discover your world and then with all your heart give yourself to it. —Buddha

10. I Am the Resurrection, I Am the Life, I Am the entrance into Eternal Light. —Jesus (From meditation)

11. When the act of reflection takes place in the mind, when we look at ourselves in the light of thought, we discover that our life is embosomed in beauty. —Ralph Waldo Emerson

12. And as we let our own light shine, we unconsciously give other people permission to do the same. As we are liberated from our fear, our presence automatically liberates others. —Marianne Williamson

13. Nothing can dim the Light that shines from within. —Maya Angelou

14. There is no blade of grass that does not have its star in heaven which strikes it and says to it: grow. — *Midrash Rabbah*, Bereshit 10:6

15. When you change the way you look at things, the things you look at change. —Wayne Dyer

16. Storms make trees take deeper roots. —Dolly Parton (Attributed)

17. What lies behind us and what lies before us are tiny matters compared to what lies within us. —Henry S. Haskins

18. Where there is great love, there are always miracles. —Willa Cather

19. With God there is no danger, Relax! —Arcturians (From meditation)

20. Try to love and live the question itself. Don't search for the answer. Perhaps then, someday far in the future, you will gradually, without even noticing it, live your way into the answer. —Rainer Maria Rilke

21. Blessed are the flexible, for they shall not be bent out of shape. —Anon

22. Women have been trained to speak softly and carry a lipstick. Those days are over. —Bella Abzug (Attributed)

My Own Quotations

23. And all will be well because All Is Well.

24. Feel the still small point deep in your heart connecting to the deep stillness of God the Mother.

25. The Universe was born in a great ecstatic orgasm of Divine Mother and Divine Father.

26. Believe in the rich juicy joy of your Divine potentiality.

27. Bask in the wonder and expectation of what is to come.

28. The password that logs you into the domain of the Father. And that password is "I choose," "I long," a cry of the heart, "I want."

29. The power of the feminine takes in, receives; providing a template for something new.

30. The important role of the masculine is to see the feminine and allow the wisdom of the feminine to adorn and inform.

31. The masculine provides protection for the birth of something new.

32. That deep still point in the heart takes you to all potentialities.

33. Let go of color. Let go of sound. Let go of shape and form. To Infinite Possibilities.

34. Beyond sound, beyond Light. Before sound there was…

35. Your Soul with God's SOUL. Be in ecstatic Peace.

36. You are Joy and curiosity. Seek the core of What Is.

37. Let go of everything you hang onto to feel safe. Go to ultimate Divine safety.

38. Let go of the need to understand and mentally latch onto something.

39. Be the peace beyond.

40. Love your body—bring Soul into HEART—Love, a golden thick liquid LIGHT, goes to every part of your body—saying, I love you, Heart, I love you, Liver—every single part of your body that you can think of —letting every single part soak, receive your Heart's love.

41. Feel your heart's golden Love. Feel yourself encased in a container of the Light of All That Is to help assimilate this Love.

42. Embody your Soul every day—walking around as a fully embodied Soul. A Soul cutting fingernails. A Soul drinking lemon tea. You, your Soul, looking at your flower. You as Soul looking at your backyard. What is it like to be a conscious embodied Soul?

43. I Am Soul Mind, I Am Soul Body, I Am Soul Heart.

44. I Am fully embodied Divine Soul.

45. I Am the Holiness of all God's creatures.

46. I Am Love fully embodied.

47. All Is Well.

48. Life Eternal is in God.

49. Enter the deep stillness and be free.

50. The Deep stillness frees from all.

51. Love is the glue, Love is the substance, Love is the structure.

52. God said, "You are Mine."

53. And God said, "Surrender to Me."

54. You are the Light of Eternal Life.

55. The Cosmic Hum (OM) is sending kisses to all at all times.

56. Radiant Sacred Sorrow is a passageway into abundant Light.

57. Bring the Sacred into Everything.

58. Be Luminous Laughter and Play.

59. Dive deep into the mire to emerge Victorious.

60. Become a Blesser. Bless Everyone all the time.

61. Become the essence of Blessing.

62. Become the vibration of Blessing, Heart, Mind, and Soul united in Blessing the World continuously.

63. Become the Love that created You.

64. Hear Divine Source calling You.

65. Luminosity is a God Job.

66. Clear the stuff that gets in your way of Love with Galactic Light Bugs.

67. Because you exist, you are Love.

68. The Universe was created by a burst of joyous laughter!

69. Bring your Soul into your Body.

Rumi

70. Stop acting so small. You are the universe in ecstatic motion.

71. Love is the bridge between you and everything.

72. You are not a drop in the ocean. You are the entire ocean in a drop.

73. I have been a seeker and I still am, but I stopped asking the books and the stars. I started listening to the teaching of my Soul.

74. By God, when you see your beauty, you will be the idol of yourself.

75. Love is the bridge between you and everything.

76. Keep silent, because the world of silence is a vast fullness.

77. Let silence take you to the core of life.

78. The wound is the place where the Light enters you.

79. Be full of sorrow, that you may become full of joy; weep, that you may break into laughter.

80. Set your life on fire. Seek those who fan your flames.

81. Dance until you shatter yourself.

82. Become the sky. Take an axe to the prison wall. Escape.

83. Let yourself become living poetry.

84. Be drunk with love, for love is all that exists.

85. I know you're tired but come, this is the way.

86. What hurts you, blesses you. Darkness is your candle.

87. You were born with wings. Why prefer to crawl through life?

88. What is planted in each person's soul will sprout.

89. The source of now is here.

90. Grace comes to forgive and then forgive again.

91. Be a lamp, or a lifeboat, or a ladder. Help someone's soul heal. Walk out of your house like a shepherd.

92. Let us carve gems out of our stony hearts and let them light our path to love.

93. Start a huge, foolish project, like Noah... it makes absolutely no difference what people think of you.

94. Whoever has heart's doors wide open, could see the sun itself in every atom.

95. The message behind the words is the voice of the heart.

96. You are not one, you are a thousand. Just light your lantern.

97. Love sometimes wants to do us a great favor: hold us upside down and shake all the nonsense out.

98. Gratitude is the wine for the soul. Go on. Get drunk.

99. I have neither a soul nor a body, for I come from the very Soul of all souls.

100. Wisdom tells us we are not worthy; love tells us we are. My life flows between the two.

101. The time has come to turn your heart into a temple of fire.

Sources Cited

Abbey of Our Lady of New Clairvaux. "Retreats." www.newclairvaux. org/visit

Allen, Scott. May 1, 2004. "New book delves into Fernald's cruel past." *The Boston Globe*. http://archive.boston.com/news/local/massachusetts/ articles/2004/05/01/cruel_past/

Angelou, Maya. 2014. *Rainbow in the Cloud: The Wisdom and Spirit of Maya Angelou*. New York: Random House.

Associated Press. January 1, 1998. "Settlement Reached in Suit Over Radioactive Oatmeal Experiment." *The New York Times*. https:// www.nytimes.com/1998/01/01/us/settlement-reached-in-suit-over- radioactive-oatmeal-experiment.html

Atticus. *Love Her Wild*. 2017. New York: Atria Books (Simon & Schuster).

Boissoneault, Lorraine. March 8, 2017. "A Spoonful of Sugar Helps the Radioactive Oatmeal Go Down." *Smithsonian Magazine*. https:// www.smithsonianmag.com/history/spoonful-sugar-helps-radioactive- oatmeal-go-down-180962424/

Cather, Willa. 1927. *Death Comes for the Archbishop*, New York: Alfred A. Knopf.

Dyer, Wayne W. 2020. *Happiness Is the Way: How to Reframe Your Thinking and Work with What You Already Have to Live the Life of Your Dreams*. Carlsbad (CA): Hay House.

Emerson, Ralph Waldo. 1903. "Spiritual Laws." *The Complete Works of Ralph Waldo Emerson Volume II*. New York: Haughton Mifflin.

Ferretti, Andrea. June 10, 2021. "A Beginner's Guide to the Chakras." Yoga Journal Online. https://www.yogajournal.com/poses/beginners-guide-chakras/

Fleming, Victor. 1939. *The Wizard of Oz*. Metro-Goldwyn-Mayer.

Freedman, H and Maurice Simon, et al. 1961. *Midrash Rabbah*. London: The Soncino Press.

Greene, Dana. Spring 1987. "Adhering to God: The Message of Evelyn Underhill for Our Times." *Spirituality Today*, Vol. 39.

Haskins, Henry Stanley. 1940. *Meditations in Wall Street*. New York: William Morrow & Company.

Hullett, Alyssa. June 21, 2021. "The Beginner's Guide to Bhakti Yoga." Greatist. https://greatist.com/health/bhakti-yoga

Kripalu Center for Yoga & Health. "The Beginners' Guide to Kirtan and Mantra." https://kripalu.org/resources/beginners-guide-kirtan-and-mantra

Liu, Eric. September 4, 2008. "Convocation Speech."

https://www.hws.edu/news/transcripts/08/convocation_liu.aspx

Lennon, John, and Paul McCartney. 1970. "Let it Be." *Let It Be*. EMI Catalogue.

Merton, Thomas. 1960. *The Wisdom of the Desert*. Trappist (KY): The Abbey of Gethsemani, Inc.

Musker, Jon and Ron Clements. 1997. *Hercules*. Walt Disney Pictures.

Rilke, Rainer Maria. 1945. *Letters to a Young Poet*. London: Sidgwick and Jackson.

Rowe, David and Robert Schulmann. 2007. *Einstein on Politics: His Private Thoughts and Public Stands on Nationalism.* Princeton (NJ): Princeton University Press.

Schaff, Philip, Ed. 1887. *A Select Library of the Nicene and Post-Nicene Fathers of the Christian Church, Volume XII Saint Chrysostom: Homilies on the Epistles of Paul to the Corinthians.* Grand Rapids: Wm. B. Eerdmans Publishing Company.

Tauro, Joseph Louis. 1993. Ricci v. Okin, 823 F. Supp. 984 (D. Mass.)

Thomas, Henry and Dana Lee Thomas. [1940] 1946. *Living Biographies of Great Composers.* Garden City (NY): Blue Ribbon.

Wickenden, Andrew. April 26, 2010. "A Place for Free Speech." *Pulteney Street Survey.* https://issuu.com/hwscolleges/docs/springpss10f/12

Williamson, Marianne. 2009. *A Return to Love.* New York: Harper Collins.

About the Author

Ann Naimark earned a BA in psychology from Hobart and William Smith Colleges. She became a massage therapist while living in Cambridge, Massachusetts. Going to Yuba College in Marysville, CA, she became an LVN and then attended an off-campus program through the Regents Program of the University of the State of New York, which led to her becoming an RN in California. She attended the University of San Francisco for her MA in counseling and has been working as a licensed marriage and family counselor (MFT) since 1993, both in mental health agencies and in her own private practice.

She began incorporating spirituality into her counseling work when clients said no one was talking about this subject in their lives. She has felt for many years that attending to and integrating body, mind, emotion, and spirit are all important, and all spiritual. And that is how she approaches her therapy work.

In addition, for many years, Ann has led meditations and taught classes in varying spiritual subjects.

Honoring our human diversity, Ann adheres strongly to the idea that there are many ways to our spiritual evolution. She honors everyone's experience and inclination and supports each person in their unique style.

Born in Camden, New Jersey, she currently resides in Sacramento, California.

Please visit her at www.annnaimark.com or send her email at annnaimark5@gmail.com. You can also visit her YouTube channel for meditations and find her on Facebook at facebook.com/ann. naimark/.

Made in the USA
Middletown, DE
27 December 2022

20516454R00146